FIRST EDITION

Designer: G. H. DeLong, Jr., DeLong and Company, Gainesville, Georgia.
Printed by Matthews Printing Company, Gainesville, Georgia.
Bindery: Nicholstone Book Bindery, Nashville, Tennessee.

ISBN 0-9655107-2-7

The Featherbone Spirit

CELEBRATING LIFE'S CONNECTIONS

CHARLES E. "GUS" WHALEN, JR.

with
PHILLIP ROB BELLURY

Foreword by
ANGUS S. KING, JR.
Governor, State of Maine

with a special contribution from **ART LINKLETTER**

This we know:

THE EARTH does not belong to MAN ,

MAN belongs to the EARTH .

ALL THINGS ARE CONNECTED like the

blood that UNITES us all:

Man did not weave the WEB OF LIFE ;

he is but a STRAND in it.

whatever he does to THE WEB he does to himself.

— CHIEF SEATTLE

is dedicated to Y O U ,

and the C O N N E C T I O N S

in your L I F E .

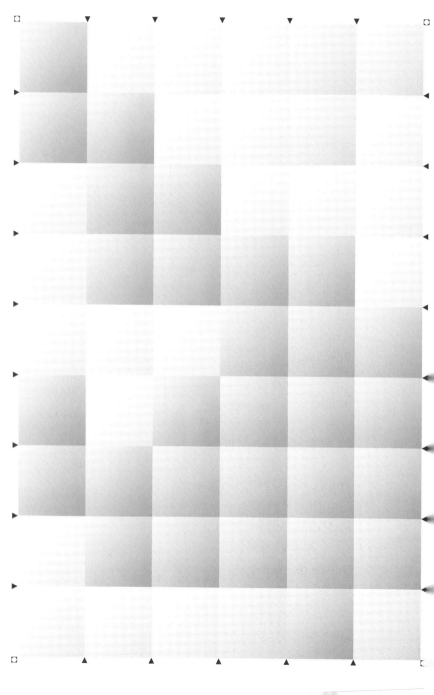

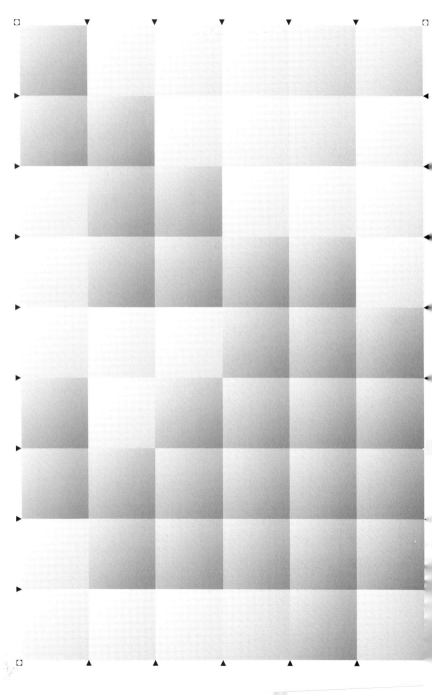

Preface

*W*hy should you read this book? Here are **three good reasons:**

In my first book, *The Featherbone Principle, A Declaration of Interdependence,* I wrote about connections in a business setting. To help illustrate the points, I drew upon my work experience in an unusual company, The Warren Featherbone Company of Gainesville, Georgia. Established in 1883, the company today manufactures baby clothes and is one of very few to have operated in three different centuries. The ideals and principles gathered from all the people and events of those years attracted many readers who also found meaning in what we wrote about. And I think they were also pleased to learn that the book was *not* the author's life story. **Reason number one — this book isn't either!**

This book, I believe, takes the idea of personal connection to a higher level. In a way, the book wrote itself. As in the first book, my role has been that of an observer. The people and circumstances that have come into my life leave lessons for all of us. For instance, my experiences in the last few years have convinced me that grandparents may be society's greatest connectors.

If it's true, then that's great news to the 78 million Baby Boomers who have become — or will soon become — grandparents. ***Reason number two — your author has been paying attention!***

This book celebrates life. In recent years, I've delivered talks and written about the power that comes from people working together. These people are interdependent within their companies. And the concept expands. Companies themselves become interdependent within their supply chains, whose sole purpose is to serve — consumers. I've discovered this is only half the story. The implications are far greater. The institutions in which we work are not only places to employ our talents; but mainly places for us to grow and get better as people. The payoff is much more than our salaries. It's *what we become* through what we do. ***Reason number three — this is your story too!***

And that's worth reading.

Gus Whalen
Gainesville, Georgia

Angus S. King, Jr., Governor, State of Maine.

Foreword

*L*ate on a Tuesday afternoon in early January of 1998, an extraordinary thing happened. It started to rain. Nothing unusual in Virginia, Kansas or Oregon, but this was Maine, and snow is what we're prepared for in winter.

What was more unusual, and ominous, was that it was colder near the ground than higher up. So as the rain fell, everything it touched was coated with a thickening veneer of ice — glistening, beautiful . . . and heavy.

And the rain continued — Tuesday, Wednesday, Thursday and through each night. By Friday morning thousands of trees and most of the power lines were down across a huge swath of Maine, and 700,000 of our citizens — about 60% of the state — were without power or heat. (Oil furnaces need an electric spark to fire, a connection many of us had forgotten.) The temperature during the week had hovered around 30, but just as the limbs and wires started to fall, it got colder, heading for single digits on Saturday morning.

Suddenly, with no warning (hurricanes seem to have a better press agent than ice storms), Maine faced its most dangerous natural disaster of modern times.

All available resources — from the utilities, the towns, the state — were mobilized. The National Guard, Red Cross, sheriffs' offices, local emergency management people, road crews . . . all were out, setting up shelters, clearing streets, feeding line crews, issuing status reports. But with the temperature dropping, it wasn't enough. We could never get to everyone, and the danger — especially to the elderly and disabled — was growing each moment the cold came on.

And then an amazing thing happened. An army suddenly appeared, in every town, village and neighborhood, on every street, and right next door. That army was made up of the people of Maine who suddenly, in the midst of crisis, rediscovered their connections to one another.

People checked in on their elderly neighbors, showed up to volunteer at area shelters, opened their homes to family, friends, and sometimes strangers, took coffee and muffins to the line crews, taught one another how to wire in generators, and, in the process, created a true community the likes of which many never experience.

In many ways, this is the essence of what Gus Whalen is talking about in this book — that life is lived at its highest level through connections, and that those connections are often forged most strongly in times of crisis and challenge.

In an age where technology and the nature of our lives

seems to push us constantly toward greater isolation and anonymity (ponder the now-common phrase "virtual community," for example), it's not a bad thing to be reminded that our very nature seeks out and depends upon connections — between friends, business associates, neighbors, families: between all of us joined in the common struggle to find purpose and meaning in our often difficult journey together.

For years, friends "from away" (as we in Maine call the rest of the world) have asked me what is so special about this place, and why I am so passionate about it. My answer is always the same: that Maine is a big small town where people know each other, care about each other, and are connected in some mysterious and wonderful way.

It's this kind of connection that Gus talks about, in Georgia, in Michigan, and across the country, and he leads us toward ways we can find and nurture these connections — even without a crisis — that so enrich our lives.

Gus didn't know it, but what he's got here is a pretty good book about Maine.

Angus S. King, Jr.
Governor, State of Maine

feath•er•bed•ding (feth' er bed' ing), *n.* a type of coercion of an employer by a labor union, in which the employer is forced to pay for services not performed, esp. by hiring unnecessary employees.

feath•er•bone (feth' er bon'), *n.* a substitute for whalebone, made from the quills of domestic fowls.

feath•er•brain (feth' er bran'), *n.* a giddy or weak-minded person. —**feth'er•brained'**, *adj.*

The Featherbone Story

long time ago in 1883, a retailer, E. K. Warren of Three Oaks, Michigan, invented a product called "Featherbone". Featherbone was a substitute for whalebone once used to stiffen women's corsets. It became the trademark of The Warren Featherbone Company, which would continuously evolve and operate a manufacturing business in three different centuries. But that's not the story.

The product Featherbone was made from turkey feather quills. These quills were discarded by feather duster manufacturers as useless byproducts. E. K. Warren recognized a use for the useless and built a company around it. The Featherbone brand name can still be found in the dictionary even though well-known brands like Chevrolet, Clorox and Pampers cannot. Unfortunately, as you see here, "Featherbone" is listed next to "featherbrain," which may explain why you haven't known about this earlier. But that's not the story, either.

A German proverb states, "Talent is born in silence, but *character* is born in the struggle of life." From day one and for quite a few years following, the company struggled to make its primary product, Featherbone, commercially viable. Once it did take hold, the product was manufactured and marketed quite successfully until 1938, when it fell prey to changing fashions and a new competitive product — plastic. All through the years, the company adapted to change and continues to do so today. Our company and others from its era did indeed develop character. In our evolution as manufacturers, we have also served as bankers, city planners, environmentalists, and publishers. As a manufacturer, we have produced Featherbone, seam binding, sewing accessories, plastic baby pants, bibs, aprons, raincoats, shoe covers, diaper bags, machine gun belts and mosquito netting (WWII), and, today, a wide variety of Alexis brand babywear . . . "made one at a time for the most precious people in the world." And, as you've guessed, that's not the story either.

As you look at The Warren Featherbone Company over time, I believe you will see that Mr. Warren's legacy has little to do with the product Featherbone. "Featherbone" is a way of thinking. Seeing the unseen. Adapting to change. Learning to be innovative and thinking long term. Most importantly, connecting to others in our lives. The Featherbone way of thinking is based on a solid set of values. These values ensure the ultimate success in the "struggle" no matter what the business is at the time. That's because the values themselves endure. In this sense, Featherbone is timely and timeless.

That's the story.

CHAPTER ONE

Heart Wednesday

**42% of all deaths are heart-related, making it
the number one killer in the United States.**
**The three major risk factors for cardiovascular
disease are heredity, increased age and male gender.**

AMERICAN HEART ASSOCIATION

ednesday, October 14, 1998. At age 53, nearly 30 years
after losing my father to heart-related disease, I met my
body on a treadmill, and it said, quietly at first, "Slow down, or
I will for both of us." Looking back on that day — and the
subsequent 96 hours — I can now see more clearly the deeper
lessons I was to learn and how it changed my life. Hopefully,
there's something you can learn from my experience without
having to live through it yourself.

In the fall of 1998, as the President and CEO of a 116-year-old, family-owned business which today manufactures infants apparel, I was a somewhat typical executive: too busy, too many commitments, not enough time in my day. And I loved it! I stayed in good physical condition by working out on a regular basis. When I traveled, I exercised in the hotel's fitness room, and at home I worked out at a fitness center at our local hospital, Northeast Georgia Medical Center in Gainesville, Georgia. This was my insurance against heart attacks — or so I thought — and it made me feel better. More energy, to go even faster!

That particular Wednesday, however, I woke up tired. I had slept fitfully through the night, excited about a big day of travel and potential accomplishment. At 6:15 a.m., I arrived at the hospital fitness center to begin my normal 30-minute workout on the treadmill. After about 15 minutes, I sensed a heavy feeling (no sharp pain) in the middle of my chest. The pain didn't go away, so I got off the treadmill and for 10 minutes tried to somehow convince myself that this was normal. A crisis was underway, but I was in denial.

Finally, yielding to my better judgement, I mentioned my condition to a bright young trainer at the center. She took my blood pressure and found it to be LOW! I had just been invited by my body to a cardiac event. You don't decline this kind of invitation, so the trainer and I walked to the emergency room two floors below.

Downstairs, I was checked in quickly and quite suddenly felt as if I were on the set of the "ER" television show. People came out of the woodwork to start the IVs and perform all manner of tests. I was given three nitroglycerine tablets, and the pain went away. Then it returned, but slightly stronger. The emergency room team, competently led by Dr. Kempler, needed to determine quickly if my heart was recovering or if they were dealing with a blood clot. Each condition would require different treatment, and we simply did not have much time. Then, by an amazing coincidence, Dr. Westermeyer, the only cardiologist in the hospital at that moment, walked into the emergency room — and my life — at *exactly* the right time! Immediately, he was able to determine that we were dealing with a clot.

My life has been blessed by humor, even in the darker hours. As soon as we knew the situation, at the height of my personal crisis, the cardiac nurse assigned to me said, "We need to give you a clot-buster shot, and those shots run $9,600." I glanced across the room at my trousers draped over the chair and considered the unlikely possibility that there was $9,600 in my wallet. But then the nurse went on to say, "However, we are participating in a study with Duke University, and if you agree, we will give you the shot for free. Sign here!" I know a good deal when I see one. I got the shot, the clot was busted and the pain disappeared. All that without emptying my wallet.

Afterwards, I was taken to the CCU (Cardiac Care Unit) where I received a low-tech, but equally potent form of healing. First I was connected to various vital sign monitors so I could be watched closely for a couple of days. As I surveyed my new surroundings and acknowledged my place in them, a very pleasant nurse walked into the room. Without a word, she proceeded to take out her lipstick and apply it liberally to her lips. She then walked over to me and planted a huge, juicy kiss right on my cheek. Smiling broadly, she said, "Dr. Hopkins (one of my best friends) asked me to give you that." Whew! Two clotbusters in one day!

Friday morning, I was transported by ambulance from Gainesville to St. Joseph's Hospital in Atlanta for a heart catheterization. One of my friends offered to carry me in a lawn chair in the back of his pick-up truck, but in the world of $9,600 shots, what's a $1,000 ambulance ride? I opted for the ambulance.

On arrival at St. Joseph's, I immediately felt at home and comfortable. I also liked the idea of a hospital being named after a saint, as opposed to the county commission. St. Joseph is well-known for performing heart procedures. I got in line for mine.

During the procedure, young Dr. Corrigan and his team found one blockage in the artery at the front of my heart. They repaired it on the spot using a stent implant. A stent is a small, latticed, stainless steel tube that is inserted into the artery to permanently keep it open. The procedure is much better than angioplasty, which allows the artery to close again over time. As it turned out, the other arteries were completely clear, and best of all, there was little, if any, damage done to the heart muscle. That's because it was treated so quickly after the "event."

The catheterization and stent implant were, for the most part, painless. Recovery was difficult in that I had to keep my right leg immobile for 13 hours as my groin healed. (That's where the catheters are inserted — ouch!) My evening nurse was Kathy Boylan, a very professional and caring person who reminded me of my late sister, Margaret. Margaret had been a nurse for 30 years and was trained at St. Joseph's. As Margaret would have done, Kathy stayed with me considerably past her normal work hours to make sure I was okay.

Remarkably, I was discharged the next day, returned home, and slept blissfully for ten hours. As the 96th hour of my ordeal ended, I was walking, talking and very grateful. I have the rest of my life to listen to my body, gain perspective and, most importantly, humbly acknowledge that on Heart Wednesday, 1998, someone with great influence wanted me to get to Thursday.

Looking back over the events of Heart Wednesday, I have to view it as a wake-up call. Although I was at risk — age, heredity and male gender — I thought I had eliminated all the other risk factors for heart trouble through exercise, good eating habits and not smoking. However, the stress was there, and my body was telling me to slow down, something I have done since. But there was more to learn than that. I believe Heart Wednesday also helped me better understand that I don't have forever. *Lesson One:* If there's something I consider important for me to do, such as writing this book, now's the time to do it. Not later, because there may not be a later.

In my previous book, *The Featherbone Principle,* a major theme emerged regarding finding opportunity in crisis. In the first chapter, I related the story of The Warren Featherbone Company and the crises my predecessors and I faced over our long history. But through every major crisis, there was always a major opportunity waiting just around the corner. *Lesson Two:* If you learn to look for opportunity in crisis, you will become adept at seeing it sooner, even as you go through it. And seeing opportunity during a crisis will help you be more aware, help you cope with the situation and maybe, as was my case on Heart Wednesday, help you to marvel — and sometimes smile — as the events unfold.

A final lesson that evolved from my Heart Wednesday

"crisis" has to do with another major theme of my last book: interdependence. Whether we realize it or not, we are interdependent and connected to each other in a number of ways. Sometimes I think The Warren Featherbone Company experienced all those years of crisis just so we could share the lessons and principles we've learned with the people to whom we're connected.

I feel the same way about Heart Wednesday. I was able to sit down and write this chapter within a day after the event, and then it took just a few minutes. Why? Probably because it had already written itself in my mind and I simply needed to record it on paper. Also, I knew that by sharing the experience I was connecting. It's important to share our experiences — and the lessons we've learned — because it can help others. It's one of the best things that can come out of a crisis situation.

Sharing is connecting. *And life flows when we connect.*

Mike Gans, one of Kent, Inc.'s co-owners, displays a "Don't Ever Give Up" card signed by Warren Featherbone employees and presented to Kent, Inc.

CHAPTER TWO

Never Give Up: The Kent Story

> "Never give up. Never give up.
> Never, never, never give up."
>
> **WINSTON CHURCHILL**

*I*n 1996, after two decades of faithful service to his company, Leo Bouley was laid off. Like so many Americans before him, Leo fell victim to a common trend in manufacturing to move production offshore to cheaper labor markets. But Leo's story has an uncommon ending. He got his job back. "How" he got his job back is interesting; but the deeper, more compelling story is "why."

The Kent story actually began in the early 50s, when Lloyd and Bernadine Dunn opened Princess Kent, a modest sewing facility on East Main Street in Fort Kent, a small town in northern Maine. A few years later, the enterprising couple sold their business to Stayon Products, who later sold to Kleinerts, Inc., in 1971. Kleinerts moved the plant across town into a vacant dance hall at Fort Kent Mills Village and, for a while, gainfully employed 60 people in the manufacture of children's sleepwear. Then, in March of 1976, due to overhead and transportation problems, the plant closed.

But a group of South Carolina investors, led by Marvin Coburn, saw the potential of the quality workforce already in place, as well as solutions to the other problems. They bought the plant, and by June of the same year, reopened under a new name, Kent, Incorporated. Sales efforts were immediately successful, and the company left the cramped conditions at Fort Kent Mills Village for a new 66,000-square-foot building on the east side of town. A week before the move, in April 1977, Leo Bouley joined the company just in time to help move equipment into the new facility.

In its new location, the company prospered. The new manufacturing facility was expanded twice, and by the mid-1980s, employment had grown to nearly 300 people. By then, the company's success had caught the eye of a large, multi-national baby foods corporation. In 1985, they purchased Kent.

For Bouley and other employees, the purchase was promising. It was a signal to them that a major company believed in their ability to produce quality products. As the company grew, more people from the Fort Kent community came to work there, including Leo Bouley's son and two daughters. Like many small towns, the company had become an integral part of the community. To a large degree, they were interdependent, each dependent on the other for their livelihood. In a real sense, the company was becoming a family of families.

CRISIS

But then came corporate changes that would eventually lead to trouble. The new owners were consolidating and merging subsidiaries, leading to the closing of as many as 15 domestic plants by the mid-1990s. In January 1996, the corporation was purchased by a large Swiss company and further consolidation occurred. Employees had nightmares that their jobs were in jeopardy. By February, layoffs began at the Fort Kent facility and by early fall, the nightmares became reality. The plant was scheduled to close in a few short months.

The imminent closing of the plant in Fort Kent was big news around the state of Maine. Regional and state officials declared it a disaster, and Governor King stated publicly that the "loss of 150 jobs in Fort Kent is the equivalent of losing 1500 jobs in Portland." In an attempt to convince the company to change its plans, those same officials discussed economic incentives to keep the plant open. But the company still said no. In November, the plant shut down and everyone lost their jobs.

For the corporation, the decision to close one of its facilities was a matter of bottom-line economics. Like so many other apparel manufacturers, the company made the determination that it's more profitable to make a product with cheaper labor. Of course, this doesn't always work, and occasionally both quality and service will suffer. There are other ways to bring affordable products to the marketplace, but it's a formidable challenge, particularly in the apparel industry. This time, the corporation's officers decided it was a challenge they didn't want to deal with, and they opted to send production of that particular clothing line elsewhere.

The shutdown presented the community of Fort Kent with a significant crisis. Overnight, Aroostook County's unemployment rate increased by 10 percent. Many families, like Leo Bouley's, were suddenly confronted with the heartbreaking likelihood that they would have to move elsewhere to find work. Adding to their frustration was the fact that, given the right circumstances, the plant could be a profit center.

A Lesson From The Past

As we've already learned, in the midst of crisis, opportunity arises. And, as is typically the case, there are always people of vision who see that opportunity and are willing to take the risk to gather it in. In this case, it was more than a few people. It was the whole community; in fact, the entire state of Maine. What transpired after November 1996 in Fort Kent has been described by those who were part of it as an "economic miracle." I prefer to think that the miracle was less about economics and more about people. People who persevered in the face of a formidable challenge. People who had already learned that being shut down doesn't mean it's over. People who decided they would never give up.

Help came from many corners, including state and local government, economic development groups, and funding from such groups as the Libra Foundation. Maine's governor, Angus King, stepped in personally to offer support. A Federal grant was obtained. State agencies made concessions. Utility companies offered reductions. Lenders offered low-interest loans. Employees agreed to return with a 5% pay cut.

Four co-owners — Peter Pinette, Mark Coburn, Mike Gans and Cindy Rachlin — accepted the responsibility of leading a new company with an old name, Kent, Incorporated. Pinette had been plant manager for 15 years. Both Pinette's and Coburn's fathers, along with Mike Gans, actually built the factory in 1976. Gans was one of the owners who had agreed to sell in 1985. Since that time he had remained in the apparel business, working in sales and marketing with Cindy Rachlin out of New York.

"The decision to close Kent was a management decision based on the economics of the situation," explains Mark Coburn. "The decision to reopen the facility was a leadership decision." That assessment may explain in part why thousands of companies have experienced similar shutdowns across the country. *Managers tend to operate within perceived limits, while leaders take us beyond those limits.* Some people can only see the danger in crisis, while others are able to see opportunity.

On February 17, 1997, barely six weeks after its closing, the plant officially reopened amid the cheers of local and state officials, workers and other supporters. Among those present was a beaming Leo Bouley, who said it was good to be back to work and added, "It's nice to see all the old faces." Faces of co-

𝔅𝔞𝔫𝔤𝔬𝔯

Fort Kent plant

workers. Faces of neighbors. Faces from the family of families who depend on Kent for their livelihood.

So why did Leo Bouley and many other former Kent employees get their jobs back? Because they, along with everyone else in the community, believed in themselves. Because they knew they could be productive, and they knew their efforts could turn a profit if someone was willing to give them a fighting chance. Ultimately, the family of families at Kent kept their jobs because, in the face of overwhelming crisis, they were not willing to give up the family. They were too connected to face the prospect of being separated. They wouldn't surrender.

Leo Bouley is one of many employees who got their jobs back when Kent, Inc. re-opened. Kent currently employs approximately 180 people, with projections of 225 by the year 2001.

Life flows through connections, especially in tenacious families.

ly News

pens amid cheer

— POSTSCRIPT —

IT'S A SMALL WORLD . . .

How I made contact with the people at Kent is indicative of the power of connections. One of the present owners of the company, Mark Coburn, was visiting his hometown of Greenville, South Carolina, when he learned about my first book, *The Featherbone Principle:*

"I was eating lunch at a sandwich shop on Main Street and struck up a friendly conversation with the owner, who asked me if I was from Greenville. I told her it was my hometown, but that I was now a partner in a company in Maine that manufactured infantswear. She said, 'What a coincidence. I just read a book written by a guy in your industry.' She told me the name of the book, and I ordered it immediately."

In my last book, Boeing CEO, Phil Condit, made the point that "there are very few chance meetings." Mark Coburn's "chance" encounter at the sandwich shop led to his purchase of the book. The book's messages about the interdependence between business and community and finding opportunity in crisis struck a chord with him, and he decided to call me personally to relate the fascinating story of Kent, Incorporated.

(By the way, the lady at the Greenville sandwich shop came by her copy of the book from her son, who had heard about it from someone he met on an airplane. It *is* a small world after all.)

CHAPTER THREE

Jesse's Tomatoes

**"We have met the greatest tomato grower
in the country."**

CARL LANGLEY, tomato counselee

*J*esse Jamerson hails from Lula, Georgia, a small town about 20 miles from Gainesville, home of The Warren Featherbone Company. For more than 41 years, Jesse has commuted to Gainesville to work in our cutting department, which he now heads. Jesse is soft-spoken but strong in stature and mind — stout, unassuming, salt-of-the-earth — with a sagacious twinkle in his eye.

Sometime in the spring of 1997, an idea was born to help "feed the 500" at Warren Featherbone by raising tomatoes somewhere on the company's property. The goal was to grow enough tomatoes to provide everyone a few "mater sammiches" during the long, hot Georgia summer. Jesse's green thumb was no secret, so we enlisted his help. He agreed to spearhead the effort. That year, he planted 20 tomato plants behind our facility alongside the tall chain link fence that separates it from the freeway.

When *you* grow tomatoes, if you do, how many do you reasonably expect to harvest per plant? 25? 35? 50? By the end of that first season, Jesse harvested 2,808 tomatoes from his 20 plants. He discarded 300 because they were too small. The final count, reviewed by Hall County agent, Gene Anderson, was 2508, or a whopping 125.4 tomatoes per plant! The yield was so phenomenally large we submitted the number to the Guinness Book of World Records in London.

That was 1997. Since then, Jesse has repeated the feat in each of the two succeeding years. And word of his success has spread. Jesse's reputation has grown until he's just about reached celebrity status. He's a tomato-growing phenomenon. In fact, his notoriety spawned a side industry. Among the merchandise offered in our Factory Outlet Store in Gainesville there are now "Jesse's Choice" T-shirts, calendars, coffee mugs, and of course, "Jesse's Choice" tomatoes.

Beyond merchandise, we also established a special day for

Jesse to provide "tomato counseling." Don't laugh, it's true. We placed an ad in the local newspaper and ran radio spots that advertised this "service" to anyone interested in raising quality tomatoes. Inside our Outlet Store, we sat Jesse down in a rocking chair and flanked him with a wheelbarrow full of tomatoes on one side and more rocking chairs on the other. People came

from near and far to see the tomato garden for themselves and to meet with Jesse. For the serious gardener, it was an honor and privilege to sit with Jesse and seek his advice. For the rest of us, it was just plain fun.

One of the many who came for tomato counseling was Chris Cosper, a bright young lady from our area of north Georgia. During her visit, we

Jesse Jamerson (standing) provides tomato counseling at Warren Featherbone.

learned she had recently left a nearby apparel manufacturing company that was closing its doors. She learned about an opportunity that was open at Warren Featherbone, and shortly after, came to work here. She now holds an important position with our company. Chris serves as yet another example of how

sowing the seeds of connections can reap a harvest of reward-ing relationships. On the surface, Jesse's tomato counseling appeared to be just an organized lark, but what emerged was something much more fruitful. For sure, we made at least one connection that day that resulted in a significant, long-term re-lationship and a wonderful addition to the Featherbone family of families.

Typically, when people first learn of Jesse's success, they want to know how he does it. To answer the question, we conducted a little research and identified a number of "Jesse Factors," or secrets of his success. It turns out that most of these factors are not secrets at all. He knows where to plant, he knows how to prepare the soil, he knows how to fertilize and water — steps that any good gardener knows. However, there are a few subtle techniques that Jesse employs that the average tomato grower would do well to note.

Take, for example, his choice of location. He selected an area behind the plant that has plenty of sunlight, and the fence is handy for tying the vines back as they grow. But the fence borders the freeway, and some of us had questions about being so close to all those automobile exhaust systems. Now, how-ever, more than a few people are convinced — and Jesse doesn't discount the possibility — that the vibrations from the cars passing by resonate with the plants, helping to stimulate their growth and productivity. Also, there's an element in the exhaust fumes that some people believe may help to advance the growth process, transforming ordinary tomato plants into "Screaming Jesses."

Then there's Jesse's insistence on record-keeping. He writes down everything. And I mean everything. From day one, he notes every detail, whether it's when and how much he fertilizes, or what days he waters, or any other activity, no matter how trivial. The first day of harvest is noted, even if it's just one tomato. Every tomato is weighed, and every tomato that doesn't fit Jesse's quality standard is discarded. For three seasons now, Jesse has recorded all the information on the progress of his tomato garden. If you've been in business long enough, or studied advanced manufacturing technologies such as "statistical process control" methods, you already know the significance of Jesse's intuitive insistence on accurate record-keeping. Come harvest time, it makes a difference.

Another "Jesse-ism" is evident when you tour the tomato garden with him. Jesse is involved. He's focused. And he loves to share his knowledge with others. He gets you involved. You can't inspect just one or two vines; you have to spend time with each one. You get to know the plants. This year he got his grandson involved and taught him how to grow tomatoes. By passing on his knowledge, Jesse was preserving wisdom learned over many years for future generations. Jesse understands the importance of *connecting the generations*.

So the evidence is clear. Jesse knows how to raise prize-winning tomatoes. But it took an inspection by the county agent for us to uncover Jesse's secret. He weighed all of the Jesse factors for himself and came to this significant conclusion. The secret isn't in the *how*; it's in the *why*. Jesse wasn't just planting tomatoes; he was growing tomatoes for all his friends and co-workers, the family of families at Warren Featherbone. Sharing his expertise, as well as his juicy red-ripe tomatoes, is his way of giving of himself to others. It's his way of connecting and leaving a legacy. A year later, we would think of Jesse as we celebrated a different kind of harvest.

Life — like a tomato on the vine — flows through connections.

Over 70 fourth-graders at Lula Elementary School participated in the first **Jesse's Choice Tomato Growing Contest**. Winners received savings bonds from the Warren Featherbone Foundation. In a question and answer session, one of the fourth-graders asked this question: "Will it hurt the tomato plant if my dog pees on it?" As Art Linkletter would say, "Kids say the darndest things!"

CHAPTER FOUR

Another Harvest

"No seed shall perish which the soul hath sown."

JOHN ADDINGTON SYMONDS

ednesday morning, July 14, 1998. Eight Warren Featherbone executives boarded a Cessna Citation jet owned
by our business partner of many years, Mercantile Stores Company. I was the last to board. We climbed quickly to 28,000
feet and streaked northward toward their headquarters and the
home of Mercantile Stores University in Fairfield, Ohio. We
were en route to a different meeting from any we had experienced in the past. No deals would be discussed, and no future
meetings would be scheduled. We all knew that this would be
the last trip. Mercantile Stores had been sold.

My mind wandered as we cruised nearly six miles above the countryside. In approximately four weeks, there would be no Mercantile Stores nor Mercantile Stores University. The people we had known, loved and worked so hard with for better than 30 years would be scattered to the four winds. This would be a difficult trip.

Technically, our company was the producer and seller of Alexis babywear, purchased by Mercantile and sold in their 107 stores. But our company's relationship with Mercantile was more than business. It always had been. Through the years, we developed a mutual support dynamic between us, an uncanny interest in seeing each other's company — and people — successful. We came to think of ourselves as *one company*. We exchanged personnel between the companies — mostly temporarily, but in one case, permanently. We published a book together. We traveled the world together, generally to share what we had learned with others and to benchmark world-class companies. We became *interdependent companies,* and the bonds of our relationship were strengthened.

The results of our relationship became legendary beyond our industry. Together we pioneered supply chain innovations for the apparel industry with the Israeli physicist, Dr. Eli Goldratt, author of the highly-acclaimed book, *The Goal.* Sales and earnings records were set for both partners. Stores within stores, known as the 777 Shops, jointly owned and operated, led the way. Seemingly, we could accomplish almost anything together. Each helped to define the other. We were connected in a big way. But in four weeks this connection was to be broken.

Or was it?

After an hour-and-ten-minute flight, we were cleared to land in Cincinnati. It was rainy and overcast. In such miserable weather, I felt as if I were on the way to a funeral. A van, sent by Mercantile Stores' Chairman, David Nichols, met our plane in an area just off the runway. In 35 minutes, we were greeted by our friends at the Mercantile Stores Headquarters in Fairfield. There and then, my sense of heaviness began to lift. A luncheon was to be given in our honor, but our first stop was a large state-of-the-art conference room. Projected on the wall at the far end of the room was a six-foot image of the logos of our two companies — a graphic reminder of our long-standing relationship.

We met for three hours to harvest and celebrate the experience of over 30 individuals involved in our partnership. In the process, we identified the seeds of that relationship that we felt were needed for meaningful future relationships. The time and place of this relationship might be ending, but the relationship, *the connection that had been made,* would not end. We were there to make sure it did not.

We actually began the meeting by talking about tomatoes — Jesse's tomatoes, of course. We agreed that Jesse's secret was the reason behind so many years of successful partnership between our companies. We had somehow sensed the "why" in each other's world. That deeper awareness had brought us together in a way that transformed business associates into true friends, whose individual goals were to help each other be successful. Our business partnership only provided the context for these more meaningful relationships. With mutual success as a goal, we broke every sales and profit record for both companies. The business success, however, was not the most important accomplishment. The really special and precious achievement was the creation of the relationships themselves. They would go on even though the current business context would not.

In harvesting our relationship with the people of Mercantile Stores, eight seeds were identified that were central to our growth together. These are seeds that can be planted by us as individuals in all relationships:

1. We sensed a ***kindred spirit*** between our companies and realized early on that this spirit was a good foundation on which to build our relationship.

2. We shared a high regard for ***integrity, mutual respect, humility and absence of fear.***

3. We believed in ***honest communication*** — constant, straight, non-manipulative. There would be no taking advantage of the other or taking that which was not yours.

4. We shared a mutual ***desire to learn.*** We allowed ourselves to think "outside the nine dots" and be willing to take the appropriate risks.

5. ***People cared about each other.*** Individuals were recognized and celebrated.

6. ***We were focused,*** building one achievement on another. We exercised persistence in execution.

7. We were personally committed to a ***shared vision***, which resulted in an empowered, inspired team that "wanted" to achieve.

8. ***We came to know and celebrate the whole person.*** This eighth factor was enabled by the previous seven. And it may be the most important.

Individually, most of us interact with others through a veneer that covers us like the thin skin of a tomato. When we identify with others through our career lives, we reveal only our exterior, the skin. Rarely do we break through it to the real person, to the values and potential for excellence that reside there. By knowing the whole person, we tap into that deep, awe-inspiring talent that is so near the source of who we are. It is a very powerful place.

Whether we grow tomatoes or great relationships, the seeds are similar in their purpose — *connecting us to our source.* In relationships, the truly good things that the seeds ultimately produce for others and ourselves are alone sufficient for the existence of the original relationship. Such was the case with Mercantile. What we became as people was far more important than what we achieved as companies. That connection was the beginning. Circumstances change; but great connections go on. They always have. And through people committed to the preservation of *values*, the world has become a better place.

CHAPTER FIVE

Ensuring Our Values

"We spend billions to insure our valuables.
Philanthropy helps us ensure our values."

DONNA BUTTS

EXECUTIVE DIRECTOR, GENERATIONS UNITED

*very day, when I round this corner and look out at the
sand dunes and the shoreline of Lake Michigan, I
am always awed by the sight. It's absolutely breathtaking. You
never get used to it.*"

Those are the words of Rich Hill, a 23-year veteran of the
Michigan Department of Natural Resources, who patrols the
2,000-acre Warren Dunes State Park every day. During his career, Rich worked at a number of state parks in Michigan, but in

recent years he has served as administrator at Warren Dunes
and the nearby 380-acre Warren Woods State Preserve. Both
parks are less than ten miles from Three Oaks, Michigan, where
The Warren Featherbone Company was founded. Land for both
parks was donated in 1917 through a foundation established by
my great-grandfather, E. K. Warren.

Today, Warren Dunes State Park boasts the largest attendance figures of any state park in Michigan, and probably the
most of any park in the Midwest. In 1999, visitor attendance
topped 1.8 million, or about 1,000 visitors per acre — an incredible statistic when compared with other parks. Even
Yellowstone National Park, with more than two million acres,
has just 3.1 million visitors per year, or an average of less than
two visitors per acre.

So E. K. Warren's gift to the state has proven to be an astonishing success. For eight decades it has provided millions of
people the privilege of enjoying some of nature's most spec-
tacular real estate. At a time when foundations were scarcely
heard of, when open land along Lake Michigan was still abundant, he somehow understood just how precious the property
would be in years to come. And just two years before his death
in 1919, he took steps to ensure that it would be protected.

"Mr. Warren was a man of incredible vision," marvels Rich
Hill, "because if he had never donated this land to public trust,

it would be lost by now to development. North and south of this property is densely developed, most of it in condominiums."

E. K. Warren was indeed a man of many accomplishments, and maybe none was so rich and enduring as his gift of land to the Michigan state park system. But what motivated him to commit such a bold and unprecedented act of philanthropy? What was the mission behind his foundation? These are questions of particular importance to us today as we move forward with plans for the Warren Featherbone Foundation of the future. In our attempt to find answers, we traveled back to Three Oaks to visit the community that benefitted so much from E. K. Warren's vision. And we did our research. In the process, we learned a lot about our predecessor foundation, but beyond that we also discovered that foundations in America have a fascinating and significant history.

THE STORY OF GIVING THROUGH FOUNDATIONS

Philanthropy has been around a long time. It probably has its roots in the ancient religions of the world, many of which encouraged some form of tithing as a means of giving to the less fortunate. While tithing in the early centuries was focused mostly on giving to individuals, Greek and Roman philanthropy grew to include the public at large. Today, because improvements in communication and transportation have created a greater awareness of hunger and disease around the world, philanthropy has become more global in its reach.

In America, Ben Franklin is generally accepted as one of the first and most important early philanthropists in the New World. In 1743, he founded The American Philosophical Society, which had many of the characteristics of a foundation, including a substantial endowment devoted to grants for research in all fields of scholarship. The first true foundation in America was established around 1800, and most foundations that followed were focused on giving charitably to the needs of specific people in poverty or physical distress.

Around 1900, the general trend in philanthropy became more research-oriented. Foundations directed their giving toward the "fundamental study of causes," rather than to specific organizations or individuals. A typical grant, for example, would provide support for research to determine the nature and cause of disease and ways in which a particular disease could be prevented, as opposed to direct support to a hospital. Instead of contributing money to buy food for the hungry, foundations provided funds for agricultural research, leading to a more abundant supply of cheaper and better foods.

It was during this period that two of the best-known philanthropists gave birth to their foundations. In 1911, Andrew Carnegie established the Carnegie Foundation, which exemplified the "new vision" of foundations. He held that the best gift to a community was a free library, then hospitals, medical colleges, parks and other public resources. In 1913, John D. Rockefeller, Sr., established the Rockefeller Foundation, whose charter included the mandate to "promote the well-being of mankind throughout the world."

During our trip to Three Oaks, we were reminded that my great-grandfather was a contemporary of these two most recognized philanthropists. Andrew Carnegie died the same year (1919) as my great-grandfather. Rockefeller died a few years later, but it is interesting to note that around this same period all of these men had reached the zenith of their business lives, having achieved ultimate success in their respective industries. But it appears that wasn't enough. They wanted something more. At this late juncture in their lives, they were compelled to give back to society, to contribute large portions of their wealth to help improve the quality of life for their fellow man. And foundations provided them the structure to do it most effectively.

E. K. Warren's foundation was Michigan's first. In fact, foundations were not recognized as legal non-profit entities in

Michigan until E. K. worked with state lawmakers to enact legislation making it so.* His efforts in that regard helped to open the door for foundations which followed. E. K. Warren was gifted. Like other industrial pioneers of his day, he could see possibilities. And when he recognized opportunities that would benefit the community, he seized them.

*Act 59, passed by the Michigan Legislature in November 1917, authorized the incorporation of foundations for the promotion of public welfare.

REBIRTH OF A FOUNDATION

During a recent trip to Three Oaks, Michigan, we learned a lot about the legacy of E. K. Warren. He is remembered as the champion of good causes. He had an uncanny ability to bring people together, to help them see themselves as a *family of families,* and to rally them together to make their community a better place. He was a standard bearer for Three Oaks, and in one memorable instance, challenged its inhabitants to prove their worth to the rest of the world. In 1899, when the U. S. government held a nationwide

The
Purpose
of the
Edward K. Warren
Foundation

THREE OAKS, MICHIGAN

Mrs. Mary Chamberlain Warren,
President.

George R. Fox,
Director.

contest to raise funds for a war memorial, E. K. Warren adopted the slogan, "Three Oaks Against the World," and led his tiny community to donate the largest per capita contribution. The first place prize, the famous Dewey Cannon*, is still proudly on display in the center of downtown Three Oaks.

*The Dewey Cannon is an ancient brass cannon of Spanish origin, which had been taken from the Corregidor Islands in Manila Bay by Admiral George Dewey during the Spanish-American War.

Like the Dewey Cannon, E. K. Warren's legacy is evident all around Three Oaks and the surrounding community. While we were there, we visited the state parks that bear his name. We saw his name on buildings and road signs. We had lunch at the Featherbone Restaurant and visited the site of the old Warren Featherbone factory. We saw firsthand how his influence and the influence of his foundation has been much more significant than the business that he operated years ago.

At one point on our visit, precisely at 12 noon, we heard a loud whistle blow the same as it did over a hundred years ago when so many residents worked at the Featherbone factory. It seemed to us that many decades after his death, and long after his business moved away, his spirit — like that long, low whistle — still permeates the community. To the residents of Three Oaks, that whistle probably serves as a constant, comforting reminder that it's still Three Oaks against the world; that they are still a family of families.

In a sense, our journey to rediscover the role of the Warren Featherbone Foundation has brought us full circle. E. K. Warren saw the need for protecting the environment decades before it became a national priority. Within 20 years of his death, everything he had accumulated, including land and cash, had been donated "for the benefit of the people." His mission, and that of his foundation, was to address the needs of people in his day. What we are attempting to do today, by giving rebirth to the Warren Featherbone Foundation, is to address the needs of people today, specifically the need to connect.

While technology and communication are making such great strides, we are still in many respects further apart than ever. The evidence is seen in our divorce rate and the higher incidences of alcoholism, suicide and fragmented families. Mother Theresa understood this truth when she said, "In the West there is loneliness which I call the leprosy of the world; in many ways it is worse than our poor in Calcutta." So the mission of the Warren Featherbone Foundation today is about reconnecting people. Reconnecting them to the values of E. K. Warren's era. Reconnecting them to the value of community, the value of serving each other's needs, and the value of preserving whatever parts benefit the whole. While E. K. Warren saw fit to preserve America's natural resources, we want to help strengthen another of America's great resources — its people — by nurturing the connections that enrich their lives.

As we proceed on our mission, we feel what my great-grandfather must have felt when he embarked on his. We are establishing a foundation whose ends have not yet been fully determined. We're still planting the seeds, and although some of those seeds have already born fruit, we cannot see all that will transpire in the days ahead. But we can look back at the work of all those foundations before us, particularly the work of our predecessor, E. K. Warren, and know it's well worth the effort.

The mission is just now coming into view, but it is very clear. We believe that helping people connect is vital . . . because *when we connect, we truly live.*

On June 28, 1900, E. K. Warren spoke at the dedication of the Dewey Cannon and said, in part, "I have all morning been wishing that I could get a glance when they celebrate the hundredth anniversary of this day. I want to see what my great-grandchildren and yours are doing that day."

In June of 2000 I was asked to speak at the 100th anniversary of the dedication of the Dewey Cannon. My remarks took the form of a letter to my great-grandfather.

LETTER TO MY GREAT-GRANDFATHER
by C. E. Whalen, Jr.
Presented on the occasion of the 100th Anniversary
of the Dewey Cannon
June 10, 2000, Three Oaks, Michigan

Dear Great-grandfather Warren,

Hundreds of people are here today to celebrate the spirit of Three Oaks represented in the Dewey Cannon. In many ways, you put your spirit in that cannon as you did in this community and in The Warren Featherbone Company where I have worked for 33 years. Three Oaks and the company have changed in the last 100 years, yet have held fast to some very important things that you gave us.

First, Three Oaks. Though I have not lived in Three Oaks since I was a little boy, I believe that you would recognize and be proud of your home town — Three Oaks still seems to be a great place to live. The population in 1900 was around 800. Today it is 1250. You described it much as our current Mayor Denny Gross does in saying that the people are friendly, warm and caring. They take pride in their community and have preserved the best of the legacy you left. Four schools (larger than the seven in your day) educate the young people. And the schools are loaded with computers. (Now the story of "computers" is a very long story. Remember how railroads came into being and helped connect us? In a way computers do the same thing. What they bring us, though, is knowledge and connection with people from all over the world.) The spiritual life is still very important here. Ten churches see to the needs of the community.

Walking down the street people still speak, and many

of the original families remain here. Families like the Donners, Martins, Sherrils, Crosbys, Hellengas, McKies and Jelineks. Many new people have come into Three Oaks, too, and that's how it has stayed vital all these years. People depend on each other and support each other in business. You always liked decentralized government that encouraged free enterprise. That thinking is alive and well.

Your gifts to the community are more important than ever. After several transitions, the township library is back in the original Warren Featherbone office building built in 1905. And the Chamberlain Memorial Museum is back, too. Warren Dunes and Warren Woods are more beautiful than ever. The Edward K. Warren Foundation, established in 1917, has enabled this property to be used by the state of Michigan in such a way that millions of people visit every year. Warren Dunes is now a state park of 2000 acres. It is the most visited State Park in Michigan and last year attracted 1.8 million people. Even Yellowstone, our nation's largest national park (2 million acres), only attracted 3.1 million people.

Now for the Warren Featherbone Company. My father, Charles Whalen, married your granddaughter, Mary Louise Chamberlain, and worked in the business until he died in 1969. The company produced Featherbone in a big way until 1938 when it was replaced by changing fashions and a new material called plastic, invented by B.F. Goodrich. You would have been proud of the people of the company as they reinvented Warren Featherbone as a producer of plastic baby pants, of all things. Great idea. In 1955, Warren Featherbone moved to Gainesville, Georgia. Lots of reasons, but very stressful for the community. Interestingly, as the company was leaving, it assisted one of its employees, Oscar Knoll, in opening a baby pant manufacturing business right here in Three Oaks. Mr Knoll was very successful and caught the attention of the Gerber Baby Foods Company. Gerber acquired the new business and built a baby pant manufacturing business, which became much larger than Warren Featherbone's.

Since 1955 Warren Featherbone has operated in Georgia, my home since age 12. We have continued to adapt to change. Baby pants have mostly been replaced by disposable diapers. Today we manufacture Alexis brand infantswear sold in department and specialty stores across the country. I am the CEO of the company and have been blessed with a wonderful family. My wife, Nell, and I have brought two great-great grandchildren of yours into this world. You'd be very proud.

In addition to continuing your manufacturing legacy, the Warren Featherbone Company has been instrumental in establishing a Manufacturing Appreciation Week in Georgia as well as in several other states. We are also re-establishing your foundation here, this time with the purpose of finding and celebrating the connections that enrich our lives.

As we celebrate the community of Three Oaks today, we remember the most valuable gifts you gave both the community and the Warren Featherbone Company. These are the values and principles that you exemplified so well and on which we have built our lives. They are and have been our *invisible* means of support. Things like the love of family, the love of nature, and a willingness to protect them long before we knew why. Values like honesty, hard work and frugality. That's the only way communities and companies like ours can survive. You taught us all about adapting to change. You did that constantly and we have, too.

And patriotism! Tomorrow is the 48th annual Flag Day parade in this community. Today we commemorate the Dewey Cannon and one of your best traits — tenacity.

We know that back in 1900 you led us in raising more money per capita than any other city in the United States for the U. S. Maine monument fund. Our reward was to be the prized Dewey Cannon. What many people don't know is that, even after winning the contest, the Navy was reluctant to give the promised cannon to us because Three Oaks was not important enough! That's when you went to Washington to petition the memorial committee and, receiving no resolution there, went to N. Y. harbor where you hired a tug to take you to the battleship to meet the Naval decision maker. The rest is what we celebrate today — compassion for a cause, pride in our community and persistence.

Perhaps your greatest contribution to us is expressed in your favorite scripture from 2 Corinthians — "For the things that are seen are temporal, but the things which are unseen are eternal." It's those unseen values and virtues which you modeled for us that remind us that E. K. Warren never left this community. Nor my family.

We love you.

Your great-grandson,

Eddie's banjo, made in 1928, once belonged to his grandfather, Charles E. Whalen, Sr.

CHAPTER SIX

The Banjo

"Our deepest fear is not that we are inadequate. Our deepest fear is that we are powerful beyond measure. It is our light, not our darkness, that most frightens us. We ask ourselves, who am I to be brilliant, gorgeous, talented, fabulous? Actually, who are you not to be? You are a child of God. Your playing small doesn't serve the world.

There's nothing enlightened about shrinking so that other people won't feel insecure around you. We are meant to shine as children do. We are born to make manifest the Glory of God that is within us. It's not just in some of us, it's in everyone. And as we let our own light shine, we unconsciously give other people permission to do the same. As we are liberated from our own fear, our presence automatically liberates others."

MARIANNE WILLIAMSON, author

My father, Charles E. Whalen, Sr., was born in Springfield, Massachusetts, in 1904. In his teens he developed an interest in music. As a young adult, he played professionally with big bands of the Tommy Dorsey and Benny Goodman era. His music took him many places near and far, including trips to Europe on cruise ships. He loved his music and the instrument through which he played — the banjo.

In 1929, my dad met Mary Louise Chamberlain, who was herself an accomplished concert pianist. They married and started a family together. In 1945, I was born into the family, which included three older sisters that I came to adore. When my father married Mary Louise he also married into a family business, The Warren Featherbone Company of Three Oaks, Michigan. To make room for this business in his life, his beautiful handmade banjo was put away in a case that would not be reopened. The remainder of his life was spent responsibly caring for everyone but himself. Sadly, he died one Sunday afternoon with the music still in him. A fine talent was laid to rest.

In 1972, three years after my father died, my son Eddie was born. He never knew his paternal grandfather and grandmother. He was an active, loving youngster with a tremendous capacity to concentrate on his interests and master his talent. When Eddie was twelve, he was drawn to music and stringed instruments, particularly the guitar. A musician friend of ours encouraged

Eddie by simply saying that, *if this was something he wanted to do, he could*. The right words at the right time changes lives, and those words of encouragement changed Eddie's.

The years that followed are now a blur. Eddie devoured music. He became very accomplished as a musician (some would say a phenomenon) and graduated with honors earning both an undergraduate degree in music as well as a masters in music composition from the New England Conservatory of Music in Boston, Massachusetts. After he graduated, Eddie stayed on for a while in Boston. He lived on Columbus Avenue and made his way as a writer of music and performer in musical groups that he himself organized. There is a world of talent in Boston, and being heard with a "unique" sound is a stiff challenge for someone just coming into his own.

Later, he came home for a summer visit. During a conversation with his step-grandmother, Doris, she left the room to retrieve from under her bed a very old case. Inside, of course, was the old beautiful banjo that belonged to my father and Eddie's grandfather. When she showed the instrument to him, he was captivated by it, as if it were a mysterious treasure . . . as if he had seen it before. From a metal label inside the case, he discovered the banjo was handmade in 1928 by a company in Boston. The address was Columbus Avenue, very near the house where Eddie lived.

Eddie took the banjo back to Boston and had it reworked and put into playing condition. As he had done before with other instruments, he then mastered this one. He called sometime later to say that his group had just played two of Boston's favorite clubs. Both had asked Eddie and his group to return for additional engagements because they really liked their "unique" sound, a sound that featured his playing of a very unusual instrument for this day and age. An instrument made in 1928. A pearl inlaid banjo that bridged two generations to reach Eddie.

As I reflect on it, I believe Eddie was assisted by his grandfather's hands stretching across time to unforgettable performances in 1998. When Charles E. Whalen, Sr., died in 1969, the music did not die in him after all. It simply awaited the day his grandson, Eddie, would open a case and pick up a legacy left by his grandfather. It was a connection between generations.

CHAPTER SEVEN

Care Where You Can

"The obscure we see eventually; the completely obvious takes longer."

EDWIN NEWMAN, news commentator

few years ago, we came face to face with the obvious. Throughout the decade of the 90s, we often heard from our retailers that more and more people were buying babywear products as gifts, and that grandparents were an increasingly large portion of that gift-giving population. That led us to the realization that grandparents were becoming a much more significant segment of our society, and we began to see the impact beyond our business. The numbers are astonishing. Today, there are approximately 60 million grandparents in the United

States, a number that increases dramatically each year as the Baby Boomers continue to age. By the year 2007, an estimated 96 million people will be grandparents — nearly one-third of the nation's population!

Dr. Roma Hanks, author of CONNECTING THE GENERATIONS: GRANDPARENTING FOR THE NEW MILLENNIUM, with Gus Whalen, Thomas Rooney and Mike Shannon.

Not only are the numbers larger, but the roles of grandparents are changing. Today's grandparents are for the most part younger, more active, and in many cases, taking on the responsibility for raising their grandchildren. Gerontologist and sociologist, Dr. Roma Hanks, offers this perspective:

"In 1900, the average life expectancy was 47. Today, that's the average age of the first-time grandparent. The average life expectancy at birth is 79 for women and 73 for men. Researchers predict that at least half of the Baby Boomers will live into

their late eighties and nineties. What does this mean for grandparenting? Just look at the math. If you become a grandparent at about 50, and you live to be about 90, then you have 40 YEARS of relationship-building with your grandchild."

So in years to come there will be more grandparents being grandparents a lot longer. The more we learned about all this, the more we realized that grandparents are in a unique position to *connect* people and families, which is what we are all about. It was a big "Ah ha!" for us that changed the way we looked at our business. Instead of just selling cute baby clothes to grandparents, we saw our opportunity to establish a personal connection with them and support them in their roles.

So we began looking at how we could best serve grandparents. How could we reach and understand them? How could we build a rapport with them and encourage them? How could we celebrate and promote what we now realize is such an important role in our culture?

What we noticed right away was that families are often separated by great distances, making it difficult for grandparents to connect with their grandchildren. Working with United Airlines and retailers like JCPenney, with whom we have been business partners since their founding in 1902, we decided to do something about it. We ran a national contest, "I Wanna See Grandma and Grandpa," in which families could win trips on the Boeing

777 to reconnect with their grandparents. The promotion was wonderfully successful, due in large part to the alignment with the long-established family values of JCPenney.

Then, in February of 1997, at a lunch meeting in Mobile, Alabama, a vision was born. The meeting was the result of a conversation I'd had a month earlier with Mike Shannon, who was then president of Gayfers Department Stores and on the board of the Business Executive Council of the Mitchell College of Business at the University of South Alabama. Earlier, we had discussed the idea of reaching out to grandparents, and he suggested we get together with Dr. Roma Hanks, whose work at the University in the fields of gerontology and sociology had led her to a greater understanding of the needs of grandparents. She already knew the statistics.

During lunch that day, we came to several conclusions and decided on a course of action. First, we would continue our research and conduct a series of focus groups to better determine what grandparents were thinking, what their needs were, and what could be done to help them meet those needs. We decided we would follow up with at least one seminar on the subject of grandparenting and invite anyone interested to attend. The seminar was scheduled for September in Mobile. Finally, we agreed that we would jointly publish a book on the subject of grandparenting, focusing on ideas for being a better grandparent leading into the new millennium. The book would be written by Dr. Hanks and published by the Warren Featherbone Foundation. To have it available for sale during the Christmas season, we set a deadline of Thanksgiving of that year. What started out as lunch became the "thirty minutes that changed our world."

In May, we conducted focus groups for grandparents. The wealth of new insights we gathered from that experience helped us understand how to structure and provide useful content for both the coming seminars and the book. With support from Mike Shannon and Thomas Rooney, a leader in Gayfers' marketing department, Dr. Hanks proceeded to write the book and plan seminars. Phil Bellury joined the team as a project leader, and the wheels were set in irreversible motion.

The September seminar — our first of many — was held in Mobile, Alabama, about the same time that the first draft of Dr. Hanks' book was completed. Both were deemed successful and served as tangible evidence that we were headed down the right path. In November, *Connecting the Generations: Grandparenting for the New Millennium* was published just in time to meet our Thanksgiving deadline, providing us with positive proof that miracles do happen! The book sales began immediately, the bulk of which occurred through promotions in Mercantile Stores and where else but the babywear department where grandparent traffic is high. Momentum was building, and we began to feel as if we were riding a wave.

By Spring of 1998, the wave felt more like a tidal wave as our efforts evolved from grass roots to major media. After discussions with a PBS affiliate in Atlanta, plans were made to produce a nationally televised special on the subject of grandparenting. A preliminary step in that process was a series of focus group meetings, held at Georgia Public Broadcasting headquarters and underwritten by Georgia State University. The focus group sessions were a milestone event, because they resulted in important insights and very significant, ongoing relationships. One of the first connections from the focus group sessions was with Susan Kelley, Dean of the College of Health and Human Sciences at Georgia State University. Susan is director of Project Healthy Grandparents, which provides a number of services to grandparents raising their grandchildren. Representatives from AARP and Generations United were present, and we learned of their efforts to inform and support grandparents on a national level. Later, we traveled to Washington, D.C., to meet with both organizations. We established new partnerships with Margaret Hollidge, Director of AARP's Grandparent Information Center and Donna Butts, who directs Generations United in their efforts to advance intergenerational understanding. *(Their contributions follow in the next chapter.)* Other key relationships were formed during the focus group sessions with sociologists, doctors, non-profit organizations and, of course, many grandparents, parents and grandchildren.

While work continued on the proposed television special, we continued to conduct seminars in five states. Our primary sponsor and partner in conducting these seminars was Dillard's Department Stores. We developed a website, www.Grandparentsconnecting.com, which provides us with a dynamic site for linking *(connecting)* to other individuals and organizations who support grandparenting. And finally, we produced a series of radio "moments" featuring brief commentaries and insights from Dr. Hanks.

CONNECTING THE GENERATIONS™
A RADIO "GRANDPARENTING MOMENT©"

By Dr. Roma Hanks

Over the last three years, I have had the opportunity to meet and talk with hundreds of grandparents who have attended the Connecting the Generations Grandparenting

Seminars. Their questions inspired me to write a number of "Grandparenting Moments" that have been recorded for use on radio and in conjunction with the book, *Connecting the Generations: Grandparenting for the New Millennium.* Here's one of my favorites:

GRANDPARENTS AS BEST FRIENDS

Have you ever been hurt when someone told a secret that you had asked them to keep? What do you do when your grandchild tells you something in confidence that you think a parent needs to know? One grandparent asked this at a seminar because he was struggling with this painful dilemma.

Grandparents tell me over and over, "I want to be the one my grandchild trusts . . . the one she can go to with her problems . . . her confidante." Being a confidante brings responsibilities — to advise with wisdom and good faith — and to be trustworthy and steadfast. Grandparents view themselves as sources of stability and continuity, both essential in any child's healthy development. If a grandchild tells you something and asks you not to tell his parents, you may find yourself caught in a conflict between the generations. Crisis counselors advise that we look at any potential harm from telling the secret. If the matter is serious, work first to get an agreement from your grandchild not to harm himself or others. Then use this opportunity to help your grandchild to develop the skills and courage to discuss the problem with parents. You can show your grandchild that effective communication can solve problems. Wise grandparents enjoy the benefits of a great relationship with their grandchildren without undermining the parent/child relationship. Remember, you and your grandchild are growing together. As your grandchild gains a confidante — so do you! The relationships you build with your grandchildren now can nurture you in old age. Love and trust flow in both directions.

As we enter into the new millennium, we wonder where the grandparenting phenomenon — the tidal wave — will take us next. We know we will continue to connect with others who are riding the same wave. People like Ernie Wendell. His book, *Grand-stories,* was published in February of 2000 by Friendly Oaks Publications in Texas. We learned about Ernie's book, a collection of grandparent and grandchildren stories, and offered our help in developing and promoting it.

Ernie Wendell provided us with a "special" perspective on grandparents:

"A special grandparent is a teacher who has encountered the stumbling blocks of life and can show grandchildren how to convert them to stepping stones. A special grandparent is a builder of confidence and character who personifies morality and leads by example and precept. A special grandparent is a dedicated listener who understands that the quickest connection to the heart of a grandchild is through the ear of a listener. A special grandparent is a healer who eases the hurts and treats the ills of life with tender and loving care. A special grandparent is an encourager who enables the grandchild to face life, accept the risks and seek the rewards.

Grandparents are for love. Special grandparents ARE love."

In March of 2000, we partnered with Generations United to present the first Warren Featherbone Foundation Award for Innovation in Connecting the Generations. The award was presented to an individual who fosters understanding and appreciation between the generations, especially grandparents and grandchildren, and connects them in creative ways that recognize the strengths in each generation. The first award was presented to Dr. Stewart Kandell, founder of Stagebridge, in Oakland, California, the nation's oldest intergenerational theatre company. Stagebridge is comprised of over 50

Dr. Stewart Kandell, founder of the Stagebridge theatre company.

actors, storytellers and volunteers (average age 70) whose purpose is to break down stereotypes of aging and encourage intergenerational contact through its drama and storytelling programs.

For better than two decades, Stagebridge has trained and supported older actors and storytellers, created original plays about intergenerational issues, and toured and performed these plays at schools, clubs and organizations, senior centers and retirement homes. It conducts an annual radio series of intergenerational storytelling and brings older adults into elementary schools as volunteer storytellers. Another Stagebridge program is the "Grandparents Tales Writing Contest," which encourages children to write stories about their grandparents. For his efforts at Stagebridge, Dr. Kandell has earned a well-deserved national reputation as a pioneer in the use of theatre to improve intergenerational relations and attitudes.

Among the submissions of nominees for the award, one in particular struck a chord with us. The nominator described her nominee as someone who exhibited the ability to "care where you can." And that's the message for all of us — as individuals, as companies, or foundations. It can easily be said that Dr. Kandell is a "care where you can" individual, but can it be so easily said about the rest of us? What about our companies — do they care where they can? Many companies employ what's referred to as "cause-related marketing," where a portion of profits are donated to charities. This certainly has done a lot of good for the communities around them. And it's been proven to be good business. But the kind of "caring where you can" that's most effective happens without expectations of an immediate return, which is the real definition of caring.

As a contemporary foundation, with a mission to help people connect, we want to take that definition seriously. We want to care where we can by encouraging and supporting grandparents who want to care where they can. We want to help generations connect with each other, and as a result, help to strengthen the very fabric of our society that is the family.

In a very real way, "caring where you can" is an opportunity to connect. *And when we connect, we truly live.*

In Honor of Art Linkletter

*T*he spirit of the grandparent is personified in Art Linkletter. Along with millions of other people, I've known of him much of my life. I laughed at the kids who "said the darndest things" on TV. He understood them, and through them, he understood me. His radio and television shows set ratings records for almost 50 years. "House Party" ran on CBS-TV and radio for 25 years. "People Are Funny" then ran on night-time NBC-TV and radio for 19 years. As an adult and parent, I read his books. He has written 23! *Kids Say the Darndest Things* is one of the best sellers of all time. It is #14 on the list of all non-fiction books published in the United States. His latest book, *Old Age is not for Sissies,* is a clever combination of wit and very practical advice. I still watch him on television and enjoy his current "Kids Say the Darndest Things" show with Bill Cosby.

During the Christmas season of 1999, I was reintroduced to Art Linkletter when I flew to Los Angeles to see him. I felt connected immediately. What I found was a man who chronologically was 87, yet he had not appreciably aged. And what a life!

Born in Moosejaw, Saskatchewan, Canada, he was orphaned as a child and then adopted by a Baptist evangelist minister, Reverend Fulton Linkletter, and his wife. The family moved to Lowell, Massachusetts, and then to San Pedro and San Diego, California. During his senior year in college, he was offered a job as a radio announcer. The rest, of course, is history. While his show business and writing careers have made him a household name, Art Linkletter has garnered just as much respect and accolades for his extensive accomplishments as a business entrepreneur.

Mr. Linkletter was thoroughly prepared for my meeting with him. He was mentally sharp, with a genuine warmth and that unmistakable light in his eyes. I asked him about his robust health. To keep in shape physically, his lifelong habits include diet (lowfat), exercise, sleep (7-8 hours nightly), no smoking and no drinking. In addition, he offered a special tip to keep in shape mentally: "Avoid whiners and catastrophizers". Now that *is* great advice!

What impressed me most was his sensitivity to family and to the role of grandparents. And he ought to know. He is many times a grandfather and great-grandfather and was once named

America's Grandfather of the Year.

I want you to know him, too, and realize what a national treasure he truly is. With that in mind, I've asked him to share something special just for us:

THE EDUCATION ONLY A GRANDPARENT CAN DELIVER

It is a truism that few things are more important to our society than the education of our young. By imparting knowledge and values from generation to generation, we hope that those who follow us will enjoy a better life. Particularly in today's busy, two-career households, grandparents can play a vital role in children's education.

Take reading, for instance. All of us have some favorite children's stories, and there's nothing quite like the thrill of sharing a story with a grandchild. There's more to it than the reading itself, which is the foundational skill for all learning. Reading a story with your grandchildren helps to make a connection with them. It's one thing to read "Winnie the Pooh," quite another to read it in grandpa's lap.

I remember well the look of wonderment on my grandchildren's faces after we would read one of Kipling's "Just So" stories, as I shared with them that it was one of their parents' favorite stories, too. And one of mine when I was a boy. That we should have a favorite story in common absolutely thrilled them and made them want to know about more of my favorites, so we could read them together.

Small children always are interested in exploring new things, and you can help to foster their curiosity and learning simply by explaining things that you enjoy. If you are a gardener, it won't take much coaxing to get a child who likes to be a helper to join you in the garden, where you can tell your grandchild about the various plants and other things. Remember, to small children many things are still new. Something as simple as a bee landing on a flower offers an opportunity to tell a child, without getting too scientific, about pollination and how bees make honey.

Some of the most important things we can teach children

aren't in any book. Every family has its own lore and history, if you will. In an age when families are likely to move not just across town but across the country, it is often a challenge to pass on the wonderful stories of generations past that help kids to understand who they are. My own grandchildren and great-grandchildren marvel at the idea that I once had a show on radio back before most people had televisions.

We can also share experiences that today's young people are fortunate not to experience. People of my generation can help bring a history lesson from school to life by just talking about World War II – not necessarily any awful battlefield experiences, but to convey the sense of duty and shared sacrifice that in that time was understood to be part of being an American.

Whether it's a favorite story or a shared family experience, grandparents can, without making a formal lecture out of it, teach children things they'll never fully appreciate if it is just given to them as part of a school lesson. I have an enormous amount of fun with my grandchildren, and I hope you do, too.

Art Linkletter

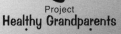

CHAPTER EIGHT

The Courage to Connect

"Children are living messages we send to a time
we will not see."

UNKNOWN

*I*n January of 2000, two Cuban grandmothers made international headlines by making a simple but courageous visit to the United States. During their visit, the grandmothers met with heads of state and religious leaders to ask our government to allow their grandson to return home to Cuba to be reunited with his father. They also met with the 6-year-old grandson, Elian Gonzales, who survived a shipwreck that claimed the life of his mother who was fleeing Cuba. The significance of that visit was not lost on all of us who value the roles of grandparents in our society and in our families. Regardless of one's position on the issue of custody, no one can deny the impact those two brave women had on public opinion. What voices could have been more powerful than Elian's own grandmothers?

Grandparents everywhere are facing issues about their roles in families. Another story that made national headlines in early 2000 revolved around the issue of visitation rights for grandparents. The issue became a court case that made its way to the U.S. Supreme Court. As more grandparents become involved in the lives of their children and grandchildren, these issues are bound to arise, especially in this age when so many people are demanding rights. While custodial and visitation rights for grandparents are still being debated, it is encouraging to note that, in most cases, grandparents are most interested in their right to give, not to get.

The connecting of a family by a grandparent takes time, effort and especially courage. More often than we realize, grandparents face the additional responsibility of raising their grandchildren. As grandparents accept this role they demonstrate to the rest of us how important it is to take the initiative in connecting, facing the fear of rejection or failure, regardless of the circumstances.

Thankfully, grandparents are not dealing with these issues

alone. There are many individuals and organizations who specifically support grandparents. Three non-profit organizations that have partnered with us are Generations United, AARP's Grandparent Information Center, and Georgia State University's Project Healthy Grandparents. These organizations are led by remarkable individuals. I want you to know them as I do and how they view their work in supporting grandparents.

DONNA BUTTS is Executive Director of Generations United, the premier national membership organization focused solely on intergenerational strategies, programs and policies.

GRANDPARENTS: CRITICAL CONNECTORS

Grandparents are the bridge from past to future. They protect and, at the same time, carry varied cultures forward, teaching the young and embracing their development with pure joy. In the best of circumstances they participate actively in their grandchildren's lives. These connections last and develop over a lifetime. My own grandpa was a valued part of my life until he passed away recently at age 95. He was independent and healthy, enjoying his 6th hole-in-one at age 86. I always made it a point to spend time with him when I was in the Midwest. He told me how much pleasure my visits gave him, and he made me feel I was important. Although on one of our last visits he said he couldn't meet me for coffee at 9 a.m. I thought he had a doctor's appointment only to find out he had an exercise class and didn't want to miss it because it was just he and "the girls"!

While there is much joy to be found in the connection between grandparents and children, there are other instances when their relationship becomes a matter of survival. Often under the saddest of circumstances, grandparents participate to a greater extent than they had ever imagined — stepping in to raise their grandchildren when parents are unable or unwilling to do so. Grandparents who are raising their grandchildren on a full or part time basis is nothing new. Unfortunately, problems such as substance abuse, illness and poverty have led to today's unprecedented increase in the number of grandparent-headed households. These grandparents are the last safety net holding the family together. Were it not for their self-less contribution and determination, millions of children would be left to the overburdened foster care system for strangers to rear. Until the passage of recent legislation, once these children reached their 18th birthday, they would be turned out on their own with no family structure to support their transition to adulthood. Grandparents who take on the demanding job of parenting the second time around not only save the family connection, they help bridge the connection between childhood and adulthood for those in their care.

Having grown up in Oregon I have a deep love for its beautiful coastline. Much of it is rugged with rock to hold back the onslaught of pounding waves. But just as much is composed of softer soil and is vulnerable to the ocean's constant encroachment. In those areas, land owners resort to rip rap — rock and wire — to try to win the battle over precious land. I think of grandparents raising grandchildren as our country's "rip rap" struggling to keep decaying families connected. As a society we don't value enough the immense contribution they make.

Our country has focused on separating the generations by creating and building single age facilities and programs. By confining young people to child-only centers and schools, we raise them to fear growing old. On the other hand, older adults who reside in senior centers often believe all young people carry guns. They hold little hope for the future and vote down local school initiatives.

Across the country, hundreds of creative intergenerational programs intentionally bring the generations together. They are based on the belief that each generation has unique strengths and should be valued. One lovely example is the New Jersey Intergenerational Orchestra, which brings together musicians of all playing levels and ages from beginner to professional and kindergartner to senior citizen. The musicians, who range from 6 to 86 years old, prove that old and young can sit side by side playing individual instruments that meld to form beautiful music.

Today, more than ever, older adults, whether grandparents by blood or spirit, are critical connectors between the generations. It's magic, simple magic, when young and old connect.

Donna Butts

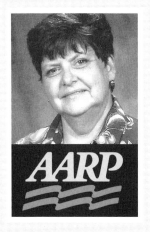

MARGARET HOLLIDGE is Senior Program Coordinator for the AARP Grandparent Information Center. The Center is an initiative of Washington, D.C.-based AARP, whose membership tops 33 million. A large percentage of that membership are grandparents. Margaret is herself a proud grandmother.

GRANDPARENTS RAISING GRANDCHILDREN

They say that having grandchildren is the reward for growing older. Most grandparents thoroughly enjoy their grandchildren, lavishing gifts, attention and affection on them at every opportunity. They delight in buying clothes and toys, in having the grandchildren over to visit and then sending them home to their parents! But for a growing number of grandparents, their grandchild's home is with them, as they find themselves taking on the parenting role for a second time. Millions of grandparents across the country are raising millions of grandchildren. Nearly 4 million children, almost 6% of children under the age of 18, are growing up in grandparent-headed households.

If asked why this is happening so much more today, most experts will point to a difficult family situation. It is true that grandparents often assume the parenting of their grandchildren in response to a family problem, usually within the parent generation. That specific problem varies. It may involve the death of the parent, financial issues around divorce and unemployment, illness, immaturity, substance abuse, or child abuse and neglect. Whatever the problem is, a gap is created in the family. Grandparents step in to fill that gap, to give their grandchildren what they need. But ask any grandparent why they do this, and the answer is love, pure and simple.

The connection between grandparent and grandchild is both unique and powerful, and it is that strong attachment that enables grandparents to face the challenges of second-time-around parenting. There are financial issues: having enough money to feed, clothe, and house the children; arranging and paying for childcare and day-care;

making sure the children get adequate medical care and a decent education. Some grandparents, like Dora, find they must stop working in order to provide the attention that their grandchildren need.

Raising grandchildren can also be complicated by the legal challenges that grandparents can face. Interacting with the courts and social service agencies can be trying for grandparents not familiar with these systems as they navigate their way through the processes of obtaining legal custody, considering foster care, and deciding between adoption and guardianship options.

Dora and Jim G. took over raising their four granddaughters, all under 6 years old, because their daughter suffered from a mental illness and was unable to consistently parent the girls. Dora decided to quit her job, not only because daycare for four children was so expensive, but because she thought they would be better off with her rather than in daycare. Not only does the family lose her current income and benefits, but Dora's future pension and Social Security benefits will also be severely reduced. Dora and Jim say, "We are their family. They belong with us."

Grandparents raising grandchildren are unsung heroes. At a point in life when careers are often at their peak, when planning for retirement is an important focus, and when time for oneself is a reasonable expectation, grandparent caregivers are faced with decisions about continuing to work, finding the money to meet the children's needs as well as their own, and setting aside personal plans to raise the next generation. But the love and safety and sense of belonging that grandparents provide their grandchildren is priceless.

Grandparents raising their grandchildren deserve all the support their communities can give them.

Margaret Hollidge

DR. SUSAN KELLEY, Dean of the College of Health and Human Sciences at Georgia State University, also serves as director of Project Healthy Grandparents, a community-based program that serves grandparents who raise grandchildren. Established in 1995, Project Healthy Grandparents was initially sponsored by Georgia State University, but is now funded with a five-year federal grant from the National Center on Child Abuse and Neglect, the Georgia Department of Human Resources, several foundations, and Georgia State. Dr. Carl V. Patton, President of Georgia State University, believes that Project Healthy Grandparents serves to connect the University with the community in Atlanta. The program is also being replicated at three other universities.

Project
Healthy Grandparents

PROJECT HEALTHY GRANDPARENTS

I began Project Healthy Grandparents out of my concern for the growing number of abused and neglected children whose own parents were incapable of caring for them. Many of these children live with their grandparents because their biological parents are substance abusers, incarcerated, deceased, or have abandoned them. Through this work, I became involved with the grandparents and was struck by the challenges they face, as well as the incredible strengths they bring to the situation. Their commitment to their grandchildren involves great self-sacrifice. Were it not for them, many of these children would be in the foster care system being raised by strangers and moved from home to home. Through the services we offer, Project Healthy Grandparents provides the support these grandparents need and deserve.

Project Healthy Grandparents' services are provided by social workers, registered nurses, tutors, and attorneys. Social workers counsel families and/or make referrals for public-assistance benefits, mental health services, health care, early childhood education, and housing issues. In addition, parenting classes and monthly support group meetings are provided for grandparents, along with transportation and child care. Registered nurses visit the families in their homes and provide health assessments and health interventions as needed. Grandparents are

screened for high blood pressure, diabetes, and high cho-
lesterol. Through a partnership with the Atlanta Legal Aid
Society, families receive free legal services regarding custody and adoption of grandchildren.

Susan Kelley

GRANDPARENTS RAISING GRANDCHILDREN
. . . SO WHAT?

The grandparenting age comes at a time of life when thoughts
turn to retirement, to settling into comfortable lifestyles, to being less involved, less connected. Many of us opt to sit on the
back pews in church, and rarely stand up to be counted. So
why, after all that, are the grandparents we've just read about
willing to step up and be counted, even in the most difficult of
circumstances? Why are they willing to sacrifice their golden
years for the sake of their children's children? What gives them
the courage?

In the final analysis, I believe these questions are best an-
swered on a spiritual level. Children really are messages we
send to a time we will not see. Grandparents understand this

truth in a way that most cannot. It provides purpose for their lives and courage in their living. They never give up. Never, ever give up. The stakes are too high. And that inspires us all.

Children are messages, and messages connect. *Life flows through connections,* and with the help of grandparents, life flows from one generation to the next.

CHAPTER NINE

Real Connections Last a Lifetime

"It's amazing how small this world really is,
when you look at it in a connecting kind of way."

WARREN FEATHERBONE EMPLOYEE

ome time ago, during a grandparenting seminar we conducted in Dallas, Texas, along with Dillard Department
Stores, we met Dick Paddock. At 79, he still retains a youthful
spirit to go along with that grandfatherly twinkle in his eye. He
had driven a long distance to make the seminar, and we're thankful he did. He taught us something about business and grandparents connecting. For you see, in 1937, eight years before I
was born, Dick worked in the accounting department at The

Warren Featherbone Company. Dick's uncle also worked at the company, as did my father, about the same time.

Dick left Warren Featherbone to join the Air Force and later retired as a Lt. Colonel in Weatherford, Texas. But through all those years in the military, he never forgot his connection to the Featherbone family. He had lost track of us until he read the advertisement in the *Dallas Morning News* announcing our grandparenting seminar. He came to the seminar certainly because he is a grandparent, but he made the trip especially because he wanted to reconnect with his corporate family of 60 years ago.

Dick Paddock never forgot his connection to Warren Featherbone and his family of families.

Dick Paddock is not the only one to feel that need to reconnect. Others have come — usually when we least expect them but always at a time that seems so appropriate in retrospect. At a meeting one Saturday morning to work on this book, we were approached by our security officer, Capt. Harold Black, who said we had out-of-town visitors. Curious, we met them in the company cafeteria and learned that 84-year-old Robert Forester and his son, Ronnie, had driven about a hundred miles from Greenville, South Carolina, on the *off chance* that someone would be here to hear his story. We were, and we did.

Robert Forester was born in Lansing, Michigan. In the 30s, as a teenager, he developed friendships with Edward and Charles Warren, who were grandchildren of my great grandfather and Warren Featherbone's founder, E. K. Warren. "You might say we were summer friends," he recalled before he went on to explain that he had photographs of the boys and himself dating back to that period. Together, we sat around the cafeteria table and searched through his scrapbook, learning about his connection to my family and my roots.

But the connection didn't stop there. Robert had more, and he was anxious to share it with us.

In my last book, *The Featherbone Principle: A Declaration of Interdependence,* I wrote about the fire that destroyed Milliken's Live Oak plant in LaGrange, Georgia. We presented that story as a great testament to the spirit of a community, a *family of families*, who pulled together during a disaster and not only weathered a storm but found unexpected opportunity in crisis. We also wrote about Roger Milliken, who led his company in its determination to make sure no one at Live Oak lost his or her job due to the fire. And no one did. One person who read that segment of the book and was especially impressed by Roger Milliken's action on behalf of his employees was Robert Forester. As it turns out, Robert worked for a number of years as a corporate pilot out of Greenville, South Carolina, and frequently flew with Roger Milliken on board.

"I knew 'Big Red' Milliken," he was proud to tell us. "A good man. When I was with Stevens Aviation in Greenville, I used to fly a lot of the Milliken people around."

During his visit to Warren Featherbone, **Robert Forrester** showed us early photos of himself and the 450 hp Spartan airplane he flew as a corporate pilot.

Robert went on to tell us about his life as an aviator, how he got his start and how he got his first ride at the age of 22 in Edward Warren's airplane. That may have been a ride that launched his career as a pilot. And Robert Forester drove the hundred miles to Gainesville just to let us know.

After these encounters with friends such as Robert Forester

and Dick Paddock, we step back for a moment and ask ourselves why they come. Why, after so many years have passed, do they still want to reconnect? Why are they willing to travel such distances, and with the risk that no one will have time to listen to their remembrances? Whatever the answers may be, we're certainly glad they took the risk, and we're glad we have the time. We are all better for it. Probably the most important accomplishment any of us make is to reconnect with the people who come into our lives in a meaningful and lasting way. A wise friend once posed this question:

"If you knew you had just one hour to live . . .

Who would you call?

What would you say?

Why are you waiting?"

CHAPTER TEN

One in the Spirit

Genetic Perspective . . .

Simply spoken, race is more of a social creation than a biological truth; therefore, using categories to divide human beings by race must be based on a source other than biology. The contemporary trend is to reject the idea that distinct races exist within the human species and acknowledge the truth that we are created by the same elemental components. The combinations of these elements are responsible for making humans incredibly similar and, at the same time, uniquely different.

MARY ANN WHALEN SCHMIDT, M.S.,

GENETIC COUNSELOR (and my daughter)

The day after Christmas 1999 our family took a very long Delta flight from Atlanta — 13 hours and 20 minutes — to Tokyo. My wife, Nell, our son, Eddie, and his new wife, Mayu, and I were on our way to celebrate the dawn of the new millennium in Fujisawa, Japan. Fujisawa is Mayu's home. Her parents, Yas and Sachiko Tsuda, had invited us to a very special occasion, an elegant concert and reception for Mayu and Eddie.

Mayu and Eddie met at The New England Conservatory of Music in Boston. Eddie, the composer/guitarist, and Mayu, the violinist, were destined to make beautiful music together. They were married in Boston in the summer of 1999 with Mayu's family attending. Now we were on the way to meet over 100 friends and relatives in Japan.

The New Year in Japan is significant in and of itself. It is their most celebrated holiday with its themes of purification and renewal. As we arrived, much of the country was shutting down, including schools, government and businesses. Millions were going on vacation, and the Buddhist temples and Shinto shrines were gearing up for New Year's visits by 90% of the entire population. On December 31, many people visit their local temples for a ceremony which focuses on the purification of one's spirit for the coming year. At exactly midnight, the giant bells of every Buddhist temple throughout Japan ring out 108 times, once for each of 108 evil passions.

So we were traveling expectantly. After a warm greeting by our new family and a day of rest, we traveled to Kamakura and the beautiful Prince Hotel, which overlooks the Pacific Ocean. The concert facility was world-class and the stage was beautifully set. I was especially pleased to see among the more than 100 guests, Mr. and Mrs. Koichi Nezu. Mr. Nezu is President of Tobu Department Stores, with whom our company has enjoyed a unique, cross-cultural relationship.

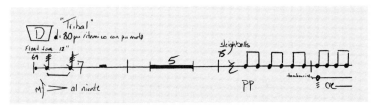

When it was time for the concert, Eddie and Mayu, accompanied by Ayako Yoda, a very accomplished pianist, created inspired music for nearly an hour. It was more than music, though. It was a union of many families and, more importantly, a union of spirit. In the highest and best sense, that's who we are — spirits. As the 20th century French philosopher Teilhard de Chardin, has written: "We should consider ourselves as spirits having a human experience, rather than humans having an occasional spiritual experience."

I tried to capture that thought in the following remarks I had prepared to close the concert..

Mayu-Ed Concert

1999年12月29日　16時開演
鎌倉プリンスホテル　バンケットルーム

プログラム

♡愛の挨拶　　　　　　　　　　　　　　　　エルガー
　　　バイオリン：真夕・ウェイレン　ピアノ：依田 彰子

♡イエス、人の望みの喜びよ　　　　　　　　バッハ
　6つのプレリュード　　　　　　　　　　　ポンセ
　やまなし　　　　　　　　　　　　　　　　津田 保治
　　　ギター：エディ・ウェイレン

♡バイオリンソナタ　変ロ長調　KV378　　モーツアルト
　　アレグロ　モデラート
　　アンダンティーノ
　　ロンド
　　　バイオリン：真夕・ウェイレン　ピアノ：依田 彰子

♡ルーマニアン　フォーク　ソング　　　　　バルトーク
　　　ギター：エディ・ウェイレン　バイオリン：真夕・ウェイレン

出演者の希望によりプログラムを一部変更させていただいております。

CONCERT BY THE SEA

Tonight we honor the marriage of Mayu Tsuda and, our son, Eddie Whalen. We also recognize that something equally wonderful is happening to their families who are also growing and changing through this marriage. In a way everyone here tonight is a part of this too, because we are all interdependent. We believe that our new family and this celebration, a concert by the sea, was meant to be. I was very impressed when  *Mayu's brother Taka, explained the meaning of the Kanji symbol for "human". We become human when we connect with another. That's what tonight is about. Connection.*

Our family is from Gainesville, Georgia, near Atlanta, and in the foothills of the Blue Ridge Mountains. My wife is Nell and we have been married 32 years — we're just getting started! We have two children, Eddie and his sister, Mary Ann. Our children have been a blessing to us as I know Mayu and her two brothers, Taka and Hiro, have been to the Tsudas. Though our family had not met the Tsudas until recently, we were already connected through the values we shared. Eddie and Mayu recognized those values first.

The beautiful music we have just heard is a reflection of

many influences. On one level it is a reflection of pure talent, musical ability and much practice. On another, and more important level, it is a reflection of love between two people. Most importantly though, what we have heard is beyond the country and culture in which those two young people have been raised. Their music is spiritual. In this sense more people than Mayu and Eddie have performed the music. Who are they? Have we met them before?

To find answers, let's look at family, and especially one of our greatest blessings — grandparents. We have lots of them. Today Japan has approximately 36 million grandparents and the U. S. 60 million. In the next 10 years this is projected to grow to 41 million and 96 million respectively — about 1/3 of our countries' populations and 1/2 of everyone over the age of 35. That's a lot of grandparents to love our children!

And grandparents have always been important as connectors of generations and communicators of values within families. Let me tell you just a little about Eddie and Mayu's grandparents. You probably have not known them, yet I think you would recognize their defining characteristics, perhaps in your families, too.

Eddie's grandparents came from the Whalen and Rollins families:

Grandfather Ralph Rollins *died this past summer and*

worked in construction most of his life. Among his defining characteristics were attention to detail and the ability to work very hard physically.

Grandmother Nell Rollins *is still living. She has been a well-respected high school teacher and is known for her sense of beauty and ability to encourage others to succeed.*

Grandfather Charles Whalen *died shortly after my wife, Nell, and I were married. He worked as president of our company. In his early adult years, though, he was a professional musician. He is remembered for his great sense of humor, unconditional love and sense of style and showmanship.*

My mother, Mary Louise, *died when I was 4 years old. She was a very talented concert pianist. My father remarried and* **Doris Whalen** *has "stepped in" to become a wonderful step-grandparent. She has great artistic talent as a painter and designer with an innate sense of balance and proportion.*

Mayu has been equally blessed:

Grandfather Toshiharu Tsuda *was a lawyer and professor at Keio University and lived in Kamakura. He passed away this year and is remembered for his discipline and sense of justice. In addition, he was a meticulous wood carver of Buddha's figure. His work — mental and physical — was precise and splendid.*

Grandmother Tazu Tsuda *is perhaps the most like Mayu.*

Though she never knew Mayu, she had a deep love of music and would have encouraged Mayu to become a musician. The Tsudas also believe she would have been pleased that Mayu married a composer, our son, Eddie.

Grandfather Shigeo Ikejima *passed away in 1972. He was a family doctor who loved people. And people loved him. He looked to nature to provide balance and perfect health.*

Grandmother Kiyoko Ikejima *passed away six years ago. She was a great lover of the arts who was very positive in her thinking. She was modern, fashionable and fun to be with. In that respect she and step-grandmother Doris Whalen would have had much in common. They never met, of course, until today. How can that be?*

Today we have heard truly beautiful music that is beyond the respective cultures of the musicians. It is a symphony. The musicians in this orchestra are, of course, Eddie and Mayu. But their hands have been guided across time by their grandparents — and all those who influenced them. ***They are the ones who have connected us through Mayu and Eddie.*** *These grandparents have met and played here tonight at this concert by the sea.*

From Eddie's grandparents we have just heard and seen:
- *precise workmanship,*
- *a sense of beauty that encourages us,*

- *style, showmanship, humor, and*
- *balance and perfect proportion.*

This symphony has also reflected Mayu's grandparents in:
- *the honesty and meticulous application of talent,*
- *the deep love of music itself and pride in the union of Mayu and Eddie,*
- *the perfect music that comes through the balance of nature with a love for people, and*
- *the music that has been artistic, positive, and life affirming.*

We have been changed by this music. It now needs to become the music of our lives. In so doing we are connected as a family of families — one in the spirit of all that is good. Life flows through connections. Only when we connect do we become "human" and truly live.

Final Thoughts . . . at least for now

Our trip together through this book brings us to a new century. A time of new beginnings to use the legacies we've been left by others. They are your gifts, too. Ways to connect and be connected.

What's in a nurse's "kiss"? Or in the family at Kent, Inc., that never gives up and never forgets — never ever? Can we connect with others, like Jesse, who knows *how*, but more importantly, *why* to grow tomatoes?

What about our relationships — do we carefully harvest and replant them? Are we visionary in our giving and thankful in our receiving? Are we ensuring our values, not just insuring our valuables? Have we been connected by grandparents and courageous in our grandparenting? In our personal relationships, are we willing to reconnect with those who have meant much to us over the years? Why do we wait?

In all these examples and so many more from your life, I believe you'll see that the common connector is the pervading presence of spirit. It's spirit that connects us to all that is good and enduring. "For the things which are seen are temporal, but the things which are unseen are eternal." **II Corinthians 4:18**

Life flows through connections. Only when we celebrate and honor the connections in our lives do we truly live today. And through spirit, forever.

ACKNOWLEDGEMENTS

In the Preface I mentioned that, in a way, this book wrote itself. That's true, but some very special people have connected to help me specifically. They are my co-authors in a very real sense, and I want you to know them:

Phil Bellury — gifted writer, researcher and friend
Nell Whalen — My wife, life partner and editor
Eddie and **Mary Ann** — my son and daughter who continue
    to teach and inspire me.

The following co-authors provided specific contributions, counsel and encouragement:

Donna Butts, Generations United
Mark Coburn and Mike Gans, Kent, Inc.
Stephanie Daniels, Three Oaks Township Public Library
Evelyn Dunagan, Nancy Flanagan, Kathryn Smith, Doris
    Whalen and **Tom Wood**, The Warren Featherbone Company
Dr. John Hardman, The Carter Center
Dr. Roma Hanks, University of South Alabama
Bill Holder, Dillard Department Stores
Margaret Hollidge, AARP

Dr. Susan Kelley and **Dr. Carl V. Patton**, Georgia State University
Angus S. King, Jr., Governor, State of Maine
Art Linkletter, television personality, author and grandparent
James Mathis, Sr., retired, Trust Company Bank of North Georgia
Jim Mathis, North Georgia Community Foundation
Jack Morgan, American Apparel and Footwear Association
David Nichols, former chairman, Mercantile Stores
Thomas Rooney, *Mobile Press Register*
Phyllis Schuler, JCPenney Company
Mike and **Maureen Shannon**, Toys "R" Us
Martha Simmons, SunTrust Bank
Owen Wells, Libra Foundation
Ernie Wendell, author, *Grand-stories*

Finally, I want to recognize the following organizations that have supported the mission of The Warren Featherbone Foundation and have made very significant financial contributions to our work:

Adams, Harkness and Hill — Boston, Massachusetts
American Hardware Manufacturers Association
    — Schaumburg, Illinois
American Production and Inventory Control Society (APICS)
    — Alexandria, Virginia
AMR Research — Boston, Massachusetts

Arthur Andersen — Atlanta, Georgia

The Boeing Company — Macon, Georgia

Brenau University — Gainesville, Georgia

Change Partners, LLC — Athens, Georgia

Computer Associates — Islandia, New York

Dillard Department Stores — Little Rock, Arkansas

Distribution America — Des Plaines, Illinois

EDS — London, England

E-3 — Marietta, Georgia

Harbinger — Atlanta, Georgia

IBM — Atlanta, Georgia

interBiz — Lisle, Illinois

Mainsaver — Woodland Hills, California

Manhattan Associates — Atlanta, Georgia

National Retail Hardware Association — Indianapolis, Indiana

PowerCerv — Tampa, Florida

Rockwell International Corporation — Milwaukee, Wisconsin

Slack Auto Parts — Gainesville, Georgia

Supply Chain Council — Pittsburgh, Pennsylvania

University of Arkansas — Fayetteville, Arkansas

University of South Alabama — Mobile, Alabama

University of Missouri — Columbia, Missouri

Walker Associates — Birmingham, Alabama

Wallace Hardware Company — Morristown, Tennessee

S P E C I A L
S U P P L E M E N T

FOUNDATIONS AT WORK

From our research for Chapter 5, "Ensuring Our Values," we learned about the extraordinary contributions of foundations toward improving the quality of life in our nation and around the world. We hope this supplement will help all of us appreciate their vital importance.

THE 10 WEALTHIEST PRIVATE FOUNDATIONS IN THE UNITED STATES

FOUNDATION LOCATION AND YEAR ESTABLISHED	ASSETS† IN BILLIONS	ESTIMATED 1999 GIVING IN MILLIONS
Bill and Melinda Gates Foundation Seattle, Washington, 1994*	$17.1	$500
David and Lucile Packard Foundation Los Altos, California, 1964	13.0	440
Ford Foundation New York, New York, 1936	11.4	550
Lilly Endowment Indianapolis, Indiana, 1937	11.1	500
Robert Wood Johnson Foundation Princeton, New Jersey, 1936	8.1	440
W. K. Kellogg Foundation Battle Creek, Michigan, 1930	6.2	221
Pew Charitable Trusts Piladelphia, Pennsylvania, 1948	4.8	230
John D. and Catherine T. MacArthur Foundation Chicago, Illinois, 1978	4.2	168
Andrew W. Mellon Foundation New York, New York, 1969	3.5	153
Rockefeller Foundation New York, New York, 1913	3.5	175

* This foundation was created this year by the merger of two other Gates foundations, founded in 1994 and 1997.
† Asset values between June 30, 1999 and August 16, 1999

Source: The Chronicle of Philanthropy

FOUNDATIONS
TODAY

Today, the philanthropic contribution to society from foundations is phenomenally high and ranks second to individual giving. In 1998, individuals accounted for $134 billion in contributions, mostly to churches and denominations. Non-corporate foundations accounted for 9.8% of overall contributions, or $17.09 billion. According to the American Association of Fund-Raising Counsel (AAFRC), non-corporate foundation giving increased by 22.9% in 1998, the third consecutive year of double-digit growth. The Foundation Center also reported that corporate foundation giving grew by 14.8% and reached $2.37 billion. Corporate foundations account for roughly one-fourth of all corporate giving.

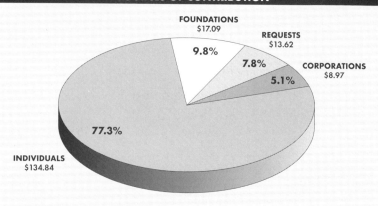

GIVING 1998: $174.52 BILLION

SOURCES OF CONTRIBUTION

FOUNDATIONS
$17.09

9.8%

REQUESTS
$13.62

7.8%

CORPORATIONS
$8.97

5.1%

77.3%

INDIVIDUALS
$134.84

NOTE: $'s IN BILLIONS

SOURCE: GIVING USA 1999 / AAFRC TRUST FOR PHILANTHROPY

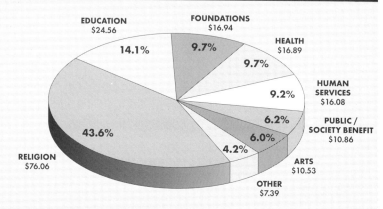

GIVING 1998

CONTRIBUTIONS RECEIVED BY TYPE OF RECIPIENT ORGANIZATION

EDUCATION
$24.56

FOUNDATIONS
$16.94

HEALTH
$16.89

14.1%

9.7%

9.7%

9.2%

HUMAN
SERVICES
$16.08

6.2%

PUBLIC /
SOCIETY BENEFIT
$10.86

43.6%

6.0%

4.2%

ARTS
$10.53

RELIGION
$76.06

OTHER
$7.39

NOTE: PERCENTAGES REPRESENT "ALLOCATED" GIVING AND ADD TO MORE THAN 100%
"OTHER" INCLUDES ENVIRONMENT / WILDLIFE, $5.25 (3.0%), AND INTERNATIONAL AFFAIRS, $2.14 (1.2%)

SOURCE: GIVING USA 1999 / AAFRC TRUST FOR PHILANTHROPY

FOUNDATIONS:
MAKING THE WORLD A BETTER PLACE

The impact of foundations on society has been quietly profound. Few of us have heard that, in 1915, the Rockefeller Foundation funded the 30-year, all-out effort to eradicate Yellow Fever. Most of us probably take for granted the convenience and accessibility of public libraries and fail to recognize the contributions from the Carnegie Foundation that made it possible. The following list summarizes a few of the more familiar contributions made by foundations over the last century. In each instance, notice how seeds of creativity and a broad concern for other people, watered and nurtured by innovation and financial resources, yield a harvest of positive change for us all.

• PUBLIC LIBRARIES

During the early 1900s, equal access to books and educational materials was revolutionary and controversial. But that didn't stop Andrew Carnegie from pursuing his vision for creating a system of public libraries. Communities from around the world requested funds from Carnegie Corporate of New York, to build libraries. By the 1920s, contributions from Carnegie and his foundation resulted in the construction of 1,679 public libraries in the United States and more than 2,500 libraries worldwide.

- **WHITE LINES ON THE HIGHWAY**

In the early 1950s, engineer-inventor Dr. John V. N. Dorr theorized that painting white lines along the outside shoulders of highways would decrease accidents. He convinced highway engineers in Westchester County, New York, to test his theory along a stretch of highway, with dramatically positive results. A follow-up test in Connecticut resulted in a similar decrease in accidents and lives saved. Dorr then used his own foundation, the Dorr Foundation of New York, to publicize the results, which eventually led to the use of state funds for painting white lines on the shoulders of highways all across the nation.

- **EMERGENCY 911**

In 1966, the National Safety Act authorized funds to create a national emergency medical response system, which provides ambulances, communications and training programs. In the early 1970s, the Robert Wood Johnson Foundation augmented this initiative by providing 44 grants in 32 states for regional emergency medical services. Following these grants, the federal government stepped in and made a series of grants that resulted in today's nationwide 911 system.

• THE HOSPICE MOVEMENT

In the early 1970s, long-term care for the terminally ill was a sad and frustrating experience for families. A group led by Florence Wald, dean of the nursing school of the Yale-New Haven Medical Center, asked foundations to fund a feasibility study for opening a hospice in New Haven, Connecticut. Simultaneous support from the Van Ameringen Foundation, the Ittleson Foundation and the Commonwealth Fund assisted in establishing and staffing a hospice to care for 100 terminally ill patients in their homes as well as in a 44-bed facility. This program became the model for hospital and home care of terminally ill patients and provided a training center for hospice workers.

• INVENTION OF ROCKETRY

In 1926, funded through a small grant from the Hodgkins Fund of the Smithsonian Institute, Robert H.

Goddard built and launched a rocket that flew 41 feet in the air for 2.5 seconds. Though many considered his efforts foolish, Harry Guggenheim took him seriously and consulted with Charles Lindbergh on the feasibility of Goddard's ideas. Lindbergh persuaded Guggenheim's father, Daniel, to provide support over a four-year period until, ultimately, the Daniel and Florence Guggenheim Foundation funded Goddard's work for 11 years. Goddard's work with rocketry was a necessary precursor to space exploration, which has in turn led to developments in satellite communications.

- **SESAME STREET**

In the early 1960s, the National Education Association endorsed the idea of making preschool education available to all children, but school budgets were insufficient for funding such programs. In 1966, the Carnegie Corporation of New York first underwrote a feasibility study on the use of television for preschool education, then gave the Children's Television Workshop a two-year grant to launch Sesame Street. Grants from the John R. and Mary Markle Foundation and others followed.

THE FIGHT AGAINST DISEASE

In the early part of the 20th Century, the spread of life-threatening, epidemic diseases became a major focus of world leaders and the public health community. Over the coming years, foundations played a major role in the battle to eradicate these diseases. Although smallpox has been the only disease to be totally eradicated, many other diseases have been all but defeated in most populations.

• YELLOW FEVER

In 1915, the Rockefeller Foundation initiated funding for fighting worldwide epidemics of yellow fever, which had already claimed tens of thousands of lives in the United States. The foundation sent physicians and scientists to cities and jungles of South America and West Africa to investigate causes. Many of these same researchers died of the fever during the course of their work, but in 1936, foundation efforts resulted in the first successful yellow fever vaccine. Millions of people were vaccinated in the years following with as much as a 90% success rate. Foundation scientist Dr. Max Theiler received the 1951 Nobel Peace Prize in medicine for his work on the yellow fever vaccine.

- **POLIO**

In 1953, Dr. Jonas Salk developed the Salk vaccine, which led to the virtual eradication of polio, a deadly and crippling disease. Salk was able to establish and equip his virus laboratory at the University of Pittsburgh through a 1948 grant from the Sarah Scaife Foundation (later known as the Sarah Mellon Scaife Foundation). Other foundations later supported Salk's work. In 1994, it was announced that polio finally had been eradicated from the Western Hemisphere.

- **THE GUINEA WORM**

In many respects, The Carter Center in Atlanta, Georgia, acts much the same as a foundation. Its funding comes in part from other foundations. Its mission is to bring people and resources together to resolve conflict, promote peace and human rights, and fight disease, hunger, poverty, and oppression around the world. Though it is involved in dozens of programs and initiatives in more than 60 countries, none may be more significant than its efforts to eradicate the dreadful disease caused by the Guinea worm.

The Guinea worm disease, or Dracunculus, has existed

for thousands of years. It is a particularly devastating disease that ultimately manifests itself in the emergence of a threadlike worm through a painful blister in the skin. Transmitted through water contaminated with tiny water fleas carrying Guinea worm larvae, Guinea worm usually affects the poorest of the poor in remote villages, mostly in Africa, India and Yemen.

In 1986, The Carter Center set a goal to eradicate Guinea worm disease. It was a bold mission. At the time, experts estimated that more than 3.2 million people were infected, with more than 100 million at risk. Eradication would require cooperation from the world's major health agencies, scientists, governments and non-governmental organizations. Working together as partners, they found solutions. Several corporations joined the battle including E.I. du Pont de Nemours & Company, which developed a special nylon fiber for water filtration. Precision Fabrics Group, another corporate partner, weaves the fiber into filters. American Cyanamid Company produces the chemical Abate, which destroys the Guinea worm larvae in water.

As a result of the visionary and compassionate efforts of The Carter Center and all of its partners, the annual incidence of the Guinea worm disease has been reduced by 95% and is headed toward complete eradication. The Guinea worm story serves as dramatic testimony to what can be done when we connect... when we direct our collective energies toward a noble cause. In this case, a life-saving cause.

TYPES OF FOUNDATIONS

There are a number of characteristics that define a private foundation. They are non-governmental and non-profit. They have a principal fund of their own and are managed by their own trustees and directors. Foundations are established to maintain or aid social, educational, charitable, religious or other activities serving the common welfare. Foundations fall into one of five classifications, each more or less self-explanatory: 1) General purpose; 2) Special purpose; 3) Family or personal; 4) Corporation (or company-sponsored); and 5) Community Foundations. Of particular interest to us are two of these types, the Community and Corporate Foundations.

- ## COMMUNITY FOUNDATIONS

Community foundations differ from other forms of

foundations in that they are more public in nature. Like private foundations, community foundations have been around for many years. The first one was established in 1914 in Cleveland, Ohio, by Frederick Harris Goff, president of the Cleveland Trust. It was essentially a partnership between the bank and community leaders. The bank trust department managed charitable endowments and a committee of citizens, chosen by representative community leaders, supervised the distribution of income to various charities.

Many people still believe philanthropy is limited to the ultra-rich. Today, however, anyone can make significant contributions through a local or regional community foundation. As a result, community foundations are increasing in popularity, with more than 500 across the nation managing thousands of "donor advised funds" for members of their communities. Most grants from a community foundation are awarded to the arts, environment, health, religion, education, human services and economic development endeavors within the community.

There are specific tax advantages for donors who give to community foundations. In addition, individual donors can relinquish all the administrative duties to the community foundation staff. While private foundations do provide more control, donors to a community foundation can make recommendations concerning the use of funds for grants or earmark donations for specific use.

- **CORPORATE FOUNDATIONS**

In recent years, corporations have contributed roughly 5-6% of overall philanthropic giving in the United States. And their contributions are growing, according to the AAFRC, who monitors giving in America. Most corporate giving is direct, but corporate foundations, who tend to give more broadly, account for more than a quarter of all corporate giving. Generally, the largest percentage of corporate contributions go to educational institutions.

In our work with Kent, Inc. (see Chapter 3), we learned about the creative efforts of the Libra Foundation, whose history and contributions to organizations and businesses in the state of Maine merit a closer look.

THE LIBRA FOUNDATION

When Elizabeth "Betty" Noyce became a year-round resident of Maine in the early 70s, she was already enormously wealthy. She wanted to share that wealth with the residents of Maine, so she established the Libra Foundation. With assets of more than $300 million, it is a very well-endowed charitable organization.

The source of those assets originated with Betty's former husband, Robert Noyce, who made technological history as the co-inventor of the integrated circuit. During the 1960s, working independently at Fairchild Semiconductor, he developed a miniaturized version of an earlier, hand-built integrated circuit that could be reliably manufactured. In 1968, he co-founded Intel Corporation, which today is one of the world's preeminent manufacturers of semiconductor memory products (chips and circuit boards).

During our study of foundations, we were pleased to learn about the role manufacturing has played in the proliferation of foundations and their resulting contributions to society. There have been a number of great names in manufacturing such as Carnegie (steel) and Ford (automobiles), who have shared their accumulated wealth through foundations. Like Noyce, their innovative manufacturing methods were considered cutting edge technology in their day.

While Robert Noyce has certainly staked a claim as one of the 20th Century's greatest innovators, much can

also be said about his wife's innovation in the area of giving. (See <u>American Heritage Magazine's</u> list on page
135.) When she first moved to Maine in 1972, Betty
Noyce contributed to causes that were closest to her heart
and closest to her immediate community in Bremen. Over
time, she increased her scope of giving to include a broader
geographical area and a more diverse range of charities.
In 1989, she created the Libra Foundation with the intent
of helping to improve the quality of life in Maine. And
although much of the Libra Foundation's grants serve traditional causes — the arts, justice, environment, education,
etc. — the real story surrounding Betty Noyce's foundation
involves her development of a non-traditional approach
to giving known as "economic philanthropy."

The basis for economic philanthropy comes from the
idea that the highest form of giving is to provide people
with employment, and much of Libra's subsequent philanthropy was designed to do just that. The first notable project
in this regard was a revitalization plan for downtown Portland. Libra's investments in the Old Port commercial dis-
trict helped stem the hemorrhaging flow of consumers to
the suburban mall complexes and brought excitement and
jobs back to the historic waterfront area. Other develop-

ments in downtown Portland were instrumental in luring big name retailers like L. L. Bean and Olympia Sports to Maine's largest city.

Libra also spearheaded other revitalization projects in other areas of the state, including two northern Maine businesses which resulted in saving literally hundreds of well-paying jobs. One of those businesses was Fresh Way, Inc., in Mars Hill, Maine, a company that had developed a unique method for processing potatoes and had begun marketing their product under the name Naturally Potatoes. But in spite of producing a high quality potato product, by early 1998 its continuing losses put the enterprise on the verge of bankruptcy. Libra decided to explore options to help save the faltering company and the jobs that would be lost as a result. They worked together creatively to find open markets for their products. Libra agreed to take a twenty percent (the maximum allowed by law) equity stake in Fresh Way and arrange for enough lines of credit to facilitate restructuring. The company then developed and marketed their unique way of preparing and shipping mashed potatoes to restaurants, with remarkable results. Mashed potatoes are showing up on more menus than ever before, because — thanks to ingenuity and resources — they taste as good as homemade!

The other business, of course, was Kent, Inc. (chapter 2), which gratefully acknowledges the role of the Libra Foundation in helping them re-organize their business. Both Mars Hill and Kent have enjoyed significant turnarounds, which offers much hope for the future of the surrounding communities where they operate. As a result of the Libra Foundation's economic philanthropy, businesses are still alive and people still have their means of livelihood.

Betty Noyce died in 1996, but her legacy continues to be showcased through a number of creative and successful programs contained within, and emerging from, the Libra Foundation. Libra's current president, Owen Wells, is a visionary in his own right and responsible for directing the organization in a manner consistent with Betty Noyce's vision. Today, the Libra Foundation continues to give in the same balanced and innovative way as always. Through the delivery of traditional grants, Libra has made many worthwhile charitable contributions; but more than that, the spirit of giving that began with Betty Noyce has literally saved a city, rejuvenated businesses and protected the jobs of hundreds, if not thousands, of people in Maine.

THE 20 GREATEST INNOVATORS OF THE 20TH CENTURY

PUBLISHED BY AMERICAN HERITAGE MAGAZINE

1. **Philo T. Farnsworth** *(1906-1971). Inventor of television.*
2. **George Washington Carver** *(1861-1943). Botanist and agricultural innovator.*
3. **Jonas Salk** *(1914-1995). Developer of a polio vaccine.*
4. **Henry Ford** *(1863-1947). Automotive pioneer.*
5. **Orville Wright** *(1871-1948). Inventor of the airplane.*
6. **Wilbur Wright** *(1867-1912). Inventor of the airplane.*
7. **Albert Einstein** *(1879-1955). Physicist.*
8. **Charles H. Townes** *(1915-). Progenitor of the laser.*
9. **Charles Steinmetz** *(1865-1923). Electrical engineer who pioneered the spread of electrical networks and the rise of the corporate research lab.*
10. **J.C.R. Licklider** *(1915-1990). Led the creation of Arpanet, which would later become the Internet.*
11. **John Von Neumann** *(1903-1957). Computer visionary, who wrote the seminal document describing the stored-program computer, the basis of today's computer industry.*

12. **William H. Gates, III** *(1955-). Personal-computing promulgator. Founder of Microsoft.*

13. **Robert Goddard** *(1882-1945). Rocket developer.*

14. **James Dewey Watson** *(1928-). Co-discoverer of the structure of DNA.*

15. **Wallace Hume Carothers** *(1896-1937). Chemist, inventor of nylon.*

16. **Rachel Carson** *(1907-1964). Marine biologist, writer, whose publication of Silent Spring in 1962 did more than any other single event to launch the environmental movement.*

17. **Willis Carrier** *(1876-1950). Inventor of air conditioning.*

18. **Gertrude Elion** *(1918-1999). Biochemist, who led in the development of breakthrough drugs against leukemia, herpes, gout, malaria, and the body's resistance to transplants. Also oversaw the development of the AIDS drug AZT.*

19. **Edwin H. Armstrong** *(1890-1954). Radio inventor.*

20. **Robert Noyce** *(1927-1990). Co-inventor of the integrated circuit and co-founder of Intel Corporation.*

ABOUT THE AUTHOR

Charles E. "Gus" Whalen, Jr. is the Chief Executive Officer of the Warren Featherbone Company of Gainesville, Georgia. In 1993, he re-established the Warren Featherbone Foundation, originally founded in 1917, to increase public awareness of the importance of interdependent connections in business and throughout society. His first book, *The Featherbone Principle: A Declaration of Interdependence*, published in 1996, has reached a wide audience and continues to be distributed through the Foundation and Amazon.com.